Tuscany
AND FLORENCE

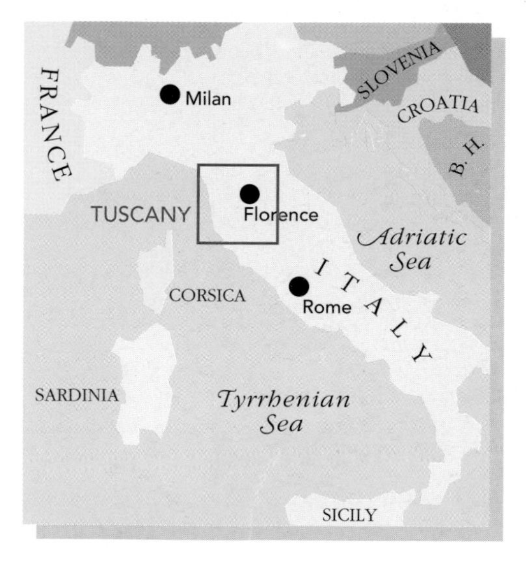

PATRICK DELAFORCE

HarperCollins*Publishers*

YOUR COLLINS TRAVELLER

Your Collins Traveller Guide will help you find your way around your chosen destination quickly and easily. It is colour-coded for easy reference:

The blue section answers the question 'I would like to see or do something; where do I go and what do I see when I get there?' This section is arranged as an alphabetical list of topics. Within each topic you will find:

- A selection of the best examples on offer.
- How to get there, costs and opening hours for each entry.
- The outstanding features of each entry.
- A simplified map, with each entry plotted and the nearest landmark or transport access.

The red section is a lively and informative gazetteer. It offers:

- Essential facts about the main places and cultural items. What is La Bastille? Who was Michelangelo? Where is Delphi?

The gold section is full of practical and invaluable travel information. It offers:

- Everything you need to know to help you enjoy yourself and get the most out of your time away, from Accommodation through Baby-sitters, Car Hire, Food, Health, Money, Newspapers, Taxis, Telephones to Youth Hostels.

Cross-references:

Type in small capitals – **CHURCHES** – tells you that more information on an item is available within the topic on churches.

A-Z after an item tells you that more information is available within the gazetteer. Simply look under the appropriate name.

A name in bold – **Holy Cathedral** – also tells you that more information on an item is available in the gazetteer – again simply look up the name.

CONTENTS

CONTENTS

PRACTICAL INFORMATION GAZETTEER

INTRODUCTION

Few regions of the world can compare with the Tuscan combination of truly beautiful countryside and renowned treasure houses. Lorenzetti's 14thC paintings show walled hill towns with towers, elegant churches and red-brick campaniles overlooking valleys of vines, olive trees, cypress and maize. If you look at the Tuscan hill towns of San Gimignano and Montepulciano today, you'll see that little has changed.

This green heart of Italy lies halfway between Rome and Milan, flanked to the west by the Tyrrhenian Sea and the mountains of the Apennines to the north and east.

There have been links between Tuscany and Britain for a thousand years. Tuscan cities became wealthy as pilgrims, having started their journey at Calais, passed through en route to Rome and the Holy Land, while in the 14th-15thC the squabbling rulers of Florence, Pisa, Lucca and Siena invited highly-trained English and Scottish mercenaries (condottieri) to contribute their skills to the savage local wars. Two centuries later, thousands of British gentry and their ladies on the Grand Tour visited 'Florence the Divine' and admired the white marble wonders of Pisa. They thought nothing of spending months studying the artistic treasures of the Palazzo Pitti and Galleria dell'Accademia di Belle Arti. During the 19thC Lord Byron, the Shelleys, the Barrett-Brownings and other literary lions, such as Henry James, Tennyson and Wordsworth, made pilgrimages to Florence to find inspiration. And now, in the late 20thC there are thousands of British settlers in Tuscany – cynically labelled 'Chiantishire' – attracted by the sheer beauty of the scenery, the friendly Tuscans, amazing culture on their doorsteps, the *cucina Toscana* and, of course, chianti classico.

The Tuscans claim not only to speak the purest Italian but also to be the most civilized of the Italian 'tribes'. The sophisticated architectural legacy of the Etruscans, dating back to 800 BC, can be seen at Fiesole, Chiusi, Volterra and Vetulonia. During the 11thC the marvellous

Romanesque churches at Pisa and Florence, Lucca and Pistoia, Prato and Carrara were built, and during the 13th and 14thC Gothic art and architecture put its unmistakable stamp on the cities of Volterra, Cortona, Pistoia, Pisa and San Gimignano. Encouraged by the Medici grand-ducal families, Tuscany, and especially Florence, became the cultural and intellectual centre of Italy (some would say of Europe). The Renaissance first flowered here in the 13thC, started by Giotto di Bondone, the painter and architect; Filippo Brunelleschi, architect and sculptor; Lorenzo Ghiberti, goldsmith and sculptor; Donatello, perhaps the greatest sculptor of the early Renaissance; and the painters Piero della Francesca and Masaccio. They were followed by the genius of Leonardo da Vinci and Michelangelo Buonarroti, and the scientific discoveries of Galileo Galilei. In addition, the literary masterpieces of Boccaccio, Petrarch and Dante astonished, amused and often scandalized their readers.

The Renaissance was a glorious period and much of this incredibly rich heritage remains in the museums, churches and *palazzi* of Tuscany. Even small hamlets have their own museums and 14th or 15thC churches, chapels and Medici villas to delight the curious visitor. Despite much damage during World War II, the scars have been skilfully repaired, and now there are more medieval traditions kept alive with colourful accuracy than in any other Italian region. The Palio delle Contrade, a superb horse race round the town square, takes place in Siena and Pistoia, crossbow tournaments are held in Volterra and Massa Marittima, there's a Saracen jousting tournament in Arezzo, rough medieval football and a traditional exploding cart in Florence, and Easter carnivals in Viareggio, Arezzo and Florence. Nowhere can you see such a brilliant, vigorous re-enactment of the past as in the towns of Tuscany.
The region, with its population of 3.6 million, is divided into the nine provinces of Arezzo, Florence, Grosseto, Livorno, Lucca, Massa Carrara, Pisa, Pistoia and Siena. Apart from the coastal plains and the

Florence

mountain ranges of the Apennines and Mugello, the rest of the countryside consists of delightful low hills with fertile valleys watered by the rivers Arno, Magra, Cecina, Serchio and Ombrone.
In addition to Florence, the capital of Tuscany, there are six areas, all very different in character. The Versilia is the coastal strip to the northwest with many miles of white sandy beaches. The Maremma is the western coastal plain of reclaimed marshland with resorts and many Etruscan sites and museums. The Chianti area is the heart of Tuscany, a large oval shape between Florence and Siena, full of wine villages, castles, abbeys and villas. The Garfagnana is the northwestern area, with the marble hills of the heavily-wooded Apuan Alps. Within its boundaries are Barga, a pretty hill village, and ramparted Lucca. The Mugello valley north of Florence was the stamping ground of the Medici in the 15thC, and it was here that they built many villas and fortresses. To the east of Florence is the unspoilt Casentino area around the upper reaches of the river Arno, with its green pastures and wooded mountain slopes.

Tuscan cuisine is among some of the best in Italy and local produce will be on restaurant and hotel menus. Chestnuts and mushrooms, superb olives and olive oil, delicacies such as wild boar, and fish from the west coast ports, all feature prominently. Many *trattorie* serve traditional meals, often flavoured with herbs, prepared to old recipes and sometimes cooked over wood fires. Accompanied by a bottle of chianti classico, a Tuscan meal becomes a memorable experience.
Holidays in Tuscany come in several guises. There are sophisticated ski resorts and scores of excellent beach resorts and marinas, plus the emerald island of Elba. The traditional spa towns of Montecatini Terme and Chianciano Terme cater for tens of thousands of Europeans seeking a cure for various ailments, and for wine-buffs the tracking down of *vino nobile* or *vinsanto,* often to be found outside the Chianti region, can be combined with the pursuit of culture, as two key wine towns are Montepulciano and San Gimignano. Archaeologists, of course, have the many Etruscan sites to explore.
However, it is still true to say that most people visit Tuscany to see the treasures of the Medici grand dukes, the Renaissance art and buildings, and the many medieval hill towns. An ideal fortnight's holiday might include a week in Florence, four or five days divided between Siena, Pisa and Lucca, and a couple of days exploring Arezzo, Volterra and Grosseto. The best time to go is in late spring or early autumn. In midsummer every town is impossibly crowded.
You will always remember the colours of Tuscany. Burnt-brick Siena, brown-sandstone Cortona, honey-coloured limestone Volterra and the bright red-tiled towers and campaniles everywhere, forming a strong contrast with the marble façades of the great Tuscan churches – green, white, red or yellow. Not to be outdone, however, it is nature which provides the dark-green cypress trees, the grey-green olives and, of course, the purple grapes of the chianti vineyards.

Ponte Vecchio, Florence

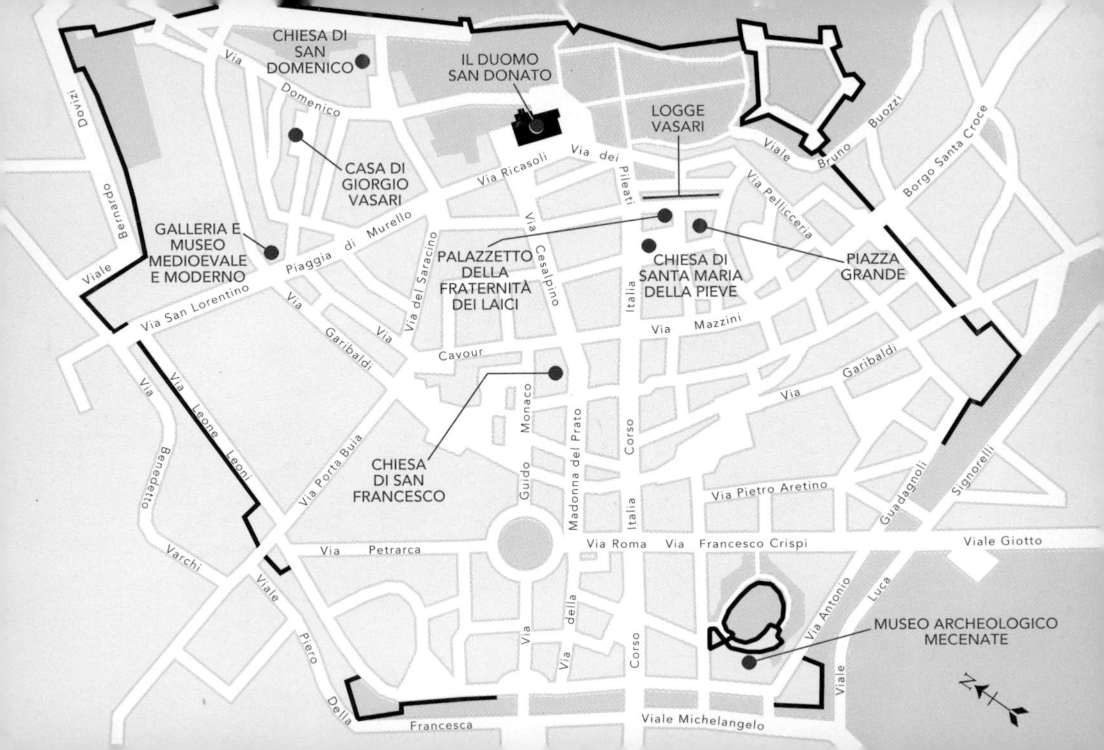
CHIESA DI SAN DOMENICO
IL DUOMO SAN DONATO
LOGGE VASARI
CASA DI GIORGIO VASARI
GALLERIA E MUSEO MEDIOEVALE E MODERNO
PALAZZETTO DELLA FRATERNITÀ DEI LAICI
CHIESA DI SANTA MARIA DELLA PIEVE
PIAZZA GRANDE
CHIESA DI SAN FRANCESCO
MUSEO ARCHEOLOGICO MECENATE
Via Domenico
Viale Bernardo Dovizi
Via Ricasoli
Via dei Pileati
Viale Bruno Buozzi
Borgo Santa Croce
Via Pellicceria
Piaggia di Murello
Via San Lorentino
Via del Saracino
Via Cesalpino
Corso Italia
Via Mazzini
Via Garibaldi
Cavour
Via Leone Leoni
Via Benedetto Varchi
Via Porta Buia
Via Guido Monaco
Madonna del Prato
Via Pietro Aretino
Guadagnoli
Signorelli
Via Petrarca
Via Roma
Via Francesco Crispi
Viale Giotto
Via della
Via Antonio
Viale Luca
Viale Piero Della Francesca
Viale Michelangelo
N

PIAZZA GRANDE East side of town.
Magnificent red-bricked square surrounded by medieval houses, 16thC arcades and galleries, the apse of Chiesa di Santa Maria della Pieve (see below) and the 18thC law courts. Note Vasari's loggia (1573) and the façade of the Palazzetto della Fraternità dei Laici.

IL DUOMO SAN DONATO Northeast corner of town.
■ Sacred art museum 0900-1200 Thu.-Sat. ● L.6000.
Huge cathedral built 1277. Note the stained-glass windows, Piero della Francesca's Magdalene *fresco (1466), Bishop Tarlatti's tomb (1330), and the della Robbia terracottas in the chapel of the Madonna of Comfort.*

CHIESA DI SAN FRANCESCO North of Corso Italia.
Beautiful remodelled 14th-18thC church with unique frescoes by Piero della Francesca of The Legend of the True Cross. *See the crib to the left as you go in. One of Tuscany's finest sights. Undergoing restoration.*

CHIESA DI SANTA MARIA DELLA PIEVE Corso Italia.
12th-14thC church with 60 m-high campanile (1330) and unusual Pisan Romanesque façade. Note Lorenzetti's Madonna and Child *above the high altar. Extensive repairs are presently under way.*

CHIESA DI SAN DOMENICO Piazza Fossombroni.
Note Cimabue altar; campanile with original bells; 15th-16thC frescoes.

MUSEO ARCHEOLOGICO MECENATE Via Margaritone 10.
■ 0900-1400 Tue.-Sat., 0900-1300 Sun. ● L.7000.
Coralline vases; 5thC Etruscan finds; 1st-2ndC Roman amphitheatre.

GALLERIA E MUSEO MEDIOEVALE E MODERNO
Via San Lorentino 8. ■ 0900-1900 Tue.-Sat., 0900-1300 Sun. ● L.7000.
Work by Aretine artists but, despite its name, nothing modern.

CASA DI GIORGIO VASARI Via XX Settembre 55.
■ 0900-1400 Tue.-Sat., 0900-1300 Sun. ● Free.
Architect, painter and sculptor's works in his own house. *See* **Vasari**.

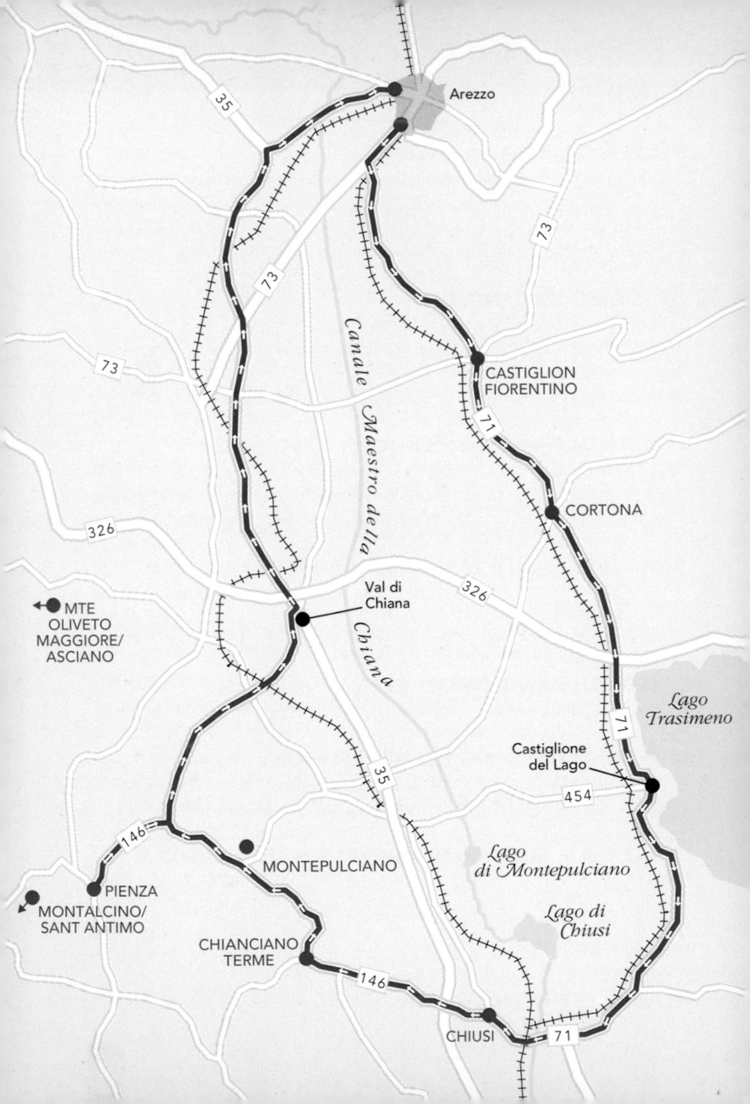
Arezzo
35
73
73
Canale Maestro della Chiana
CASTIGLION FIORENTINO
71
CORTONA
326
326
Val di Chiana
MTE OLIVETO MAGGIORE/ ASCIANO
Lago Trasimeno
71
Castiglione del Lago
454
35
146
MONTEPULCIANO
Lago di Montepulciano
Lago di Chiusi
PIENZA
MONTALCINO/ SANT ANTIMO
CHIANCIANO TERME
146
CHIUSI
71

Excursion

A one- or two-day excursion to Cortona, Montepulciano and Pienza.

Leave Arezzo past the station on Via Vittorio Veneto, head southwest and take the SS 71 signposted Cortona.
17 km – Castiglion Fiorentino. Pop: 11,000. A walled market town and centre of the Valdichiana area. In the central Piazza del Municipio is the Loggia del Vasari (1560). From the top of the 11thC castle keep you can see Mte Amiata 80 km to the southwest. The Palazzo Comunale (0900-1200 Mon.-Sat., 1600-1800 Thu.-Sat., 1030-1130 Sun.; L.3000) and the collegiate church of San Francesco have paintings and frescoes by della Gatta and Signorelli (see **A-Z**). After 14 km, on the outskirts of Cortona, is the 7thC BC Melone del Sodo, a huge Etruscan tomb.
32 km – Cortona (see **A-Z**). Drive up the winding road towards this old Etruscan hill town, from where there are superb views. After seeing the sights, go down the hill past the church of San Domenico and take the SS 71 along the shore of Lago Trasimeno, where Hannibal defeated the Roman army in 217 BC, through Castiglione del Lago (in Umbria province). Follow the course of the railway for 28 km, then take a turning to the right.
67 km – Chiusi. Pop: 9000. Once an important Etruscan city, known originally as Chamas, Chiusi was founded in the 8thC BC and has the 12thC cathedral of San Secondiano and the Museo Nazionale Etrusco (0900-1300, 1400-2000 Tue.-Sat., 0900-1300 Sun.; L.4000), both in the Piazza del Duomo. There are several notable Etruscan tombs in the town suburbs, including della Pellegrina, della Scimmia (monkey), del Granduca, Bonci Casuccini and delle Tassinaie. Guided visits to these are available from the Museo Nazionale Etrusco. Leave Chiusi on the SS 146 and go west for 12 km over the Rome–Florence autostrada to the spa town of Chianciano Terme (pop: 7300). The old walled hill town overlooks the modern spa – one of the most important in Italy with 200 hotels and boarding houses – which is very busy in the April-Nov. season. Horace and other famous Romans took the cure here for liver and gall bladder complaints. Keep northwest on the winding N 146 for 10 km.
89 km – Montepulciano (see **A-Z**). A most beautiful small Renaissance

Montepulciano

hill-top town. Leave your car outside the town gates and be prepared to walk gently uphill for 1.5 km along the Corso to the marvellous Piazza Grande. Continue west on the SS 146 for 13 km.

102 km – Pienza (see **A-Z**). A perfect little Renaissance town rebuilt in 1459 for Pope Pius II. There is now a choice:

Either: Spend the night in Pienza and then explore Sant'Antimo (see **Abbeys**) and Montalcino (see **A-Z**) to the west, or Mte Oliveto Maggiore (see **Abbeys**) and Asciano to the north.

Or: Retrace your route along the SS 146 and after 6 km take the SS 327 for 17 km northeast to join the autostrada to Arezzo at the Val di Chiana entry point. It is then 38 km back to Arezzo (163 km).

Fortezza Medicea, Cortona

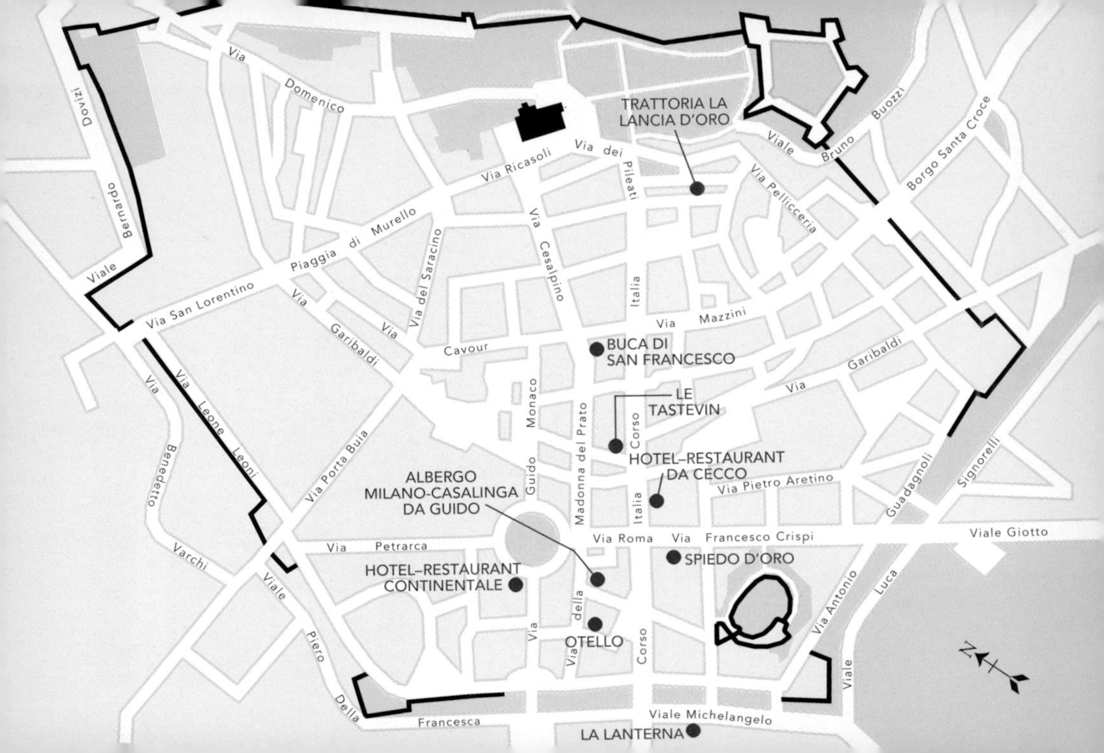
TRATTORIA LA LANCIA D'ORO
BUCA DI SAN FRANCESCO
LE TASTEVIN
HOTEL-RESTAURANT DA CECCO
ALBERGO MILANO-CASALINGA DA GUIDO
SPIEDO D'ORO
HOTEL-RESTAURANT CONTINENTALE
OTELLO
LA LANTERNA
N
Via Domenico
Viale Bernardo Dovizi
Via Ricasoli
Via dei Pileati
Viale Bruno Buozzi
Borgo Santa Croce
Via Pellicceria
Piaggia di Murello
Via del Saracino
Via Cesalpino
Via San Lorentino
Via Garibaldi
Cavour
Via Mazzini
Corso Italia
Via Garibaldi
Via Leone Leoni
Via Benedetto Varchi
Via Porta Buia
Guido Monaco
Madonna del Prato
Via Pietro Aretino
Guadagnoli
Signorelli
Via Petrarca
Via Roma
Via Francesco Crispi
Viale Giotto
Via della
Via Antonio
Viale Luca
Viale Piero Della Francesca
Viale Michelangelo

Restaurants

BUCA DI SAN FRANCESCO Via San Francesco 1.
■ 1200-1430, 1900-2130 Wed.-Sun. Closed July. ● Expensive.
This hole-in-the-wall establishment has good Tuscan cuisine and wines.

TRATTORIA LA LANCIA D'ORO Piazze Grande 18-19.
■ 1200-1430, 1900-2100 Tue.-Sun. ● Moderate.
Elegant restaurant in Loggia Vasari arcade. Osso bucco *is recommended.*

HOTEL-RESTAURANT CONTINENTALE Piazza Guido Monaco.
■ 1300-1500, 2030-2230 Sat.-Thu. Closed July. ● Moderate.
Reliable Italian cuisine; a favourite with local businessmen.

HOTEL-RESTAURANT DA CECCO Corso Italia 215.
■ 1245-1500, 2000-2215. ● Moderate.
Excellent cuisine, including Tuscan specialities, in uninspiring building.

LE TASTEVIN Via de' Cenci 9, tel: 28304.
■ 1315-1515, 2030-2330 Tue.-Sun. Closed Aug. ● Moderate.
Hidden in a side street, bookings are required for this popular restaurant.

SPIEDO D'ORO Via Francesco Crispi 12.
■ 1330-1500, 2015-2215 Fri.-Wed. Closed early July. ● Moderate.
Unpretentious restaurant serving very good Tuscan beef and goat dishes.

LA LANTERNA Viale Michelangelo 54.
■ 1300-1445, 2000-2200 Wed.-Sun. ● Moderate.
A smart Tuscan restaurant with a wide choice of mainly pasta dishes.

OTELLO Piazza Risorgimento 16.
■ 1300-1500, 2000-2200 Tue.-Sun. ● Inexpensive.
Try the crostone Otello *or* tegemaccio, *as well as the pasta and pizzas.*

ALBERGO MILANO-CASALINGA DA GUIDO
Via della Madonna del Prato 85.
■ 1300-1500, 2000-2200 Wed.-Mon. ● Inexpensive.
Simple, plain Tuscan fare; no trimmings but a pleasant atmosphere.

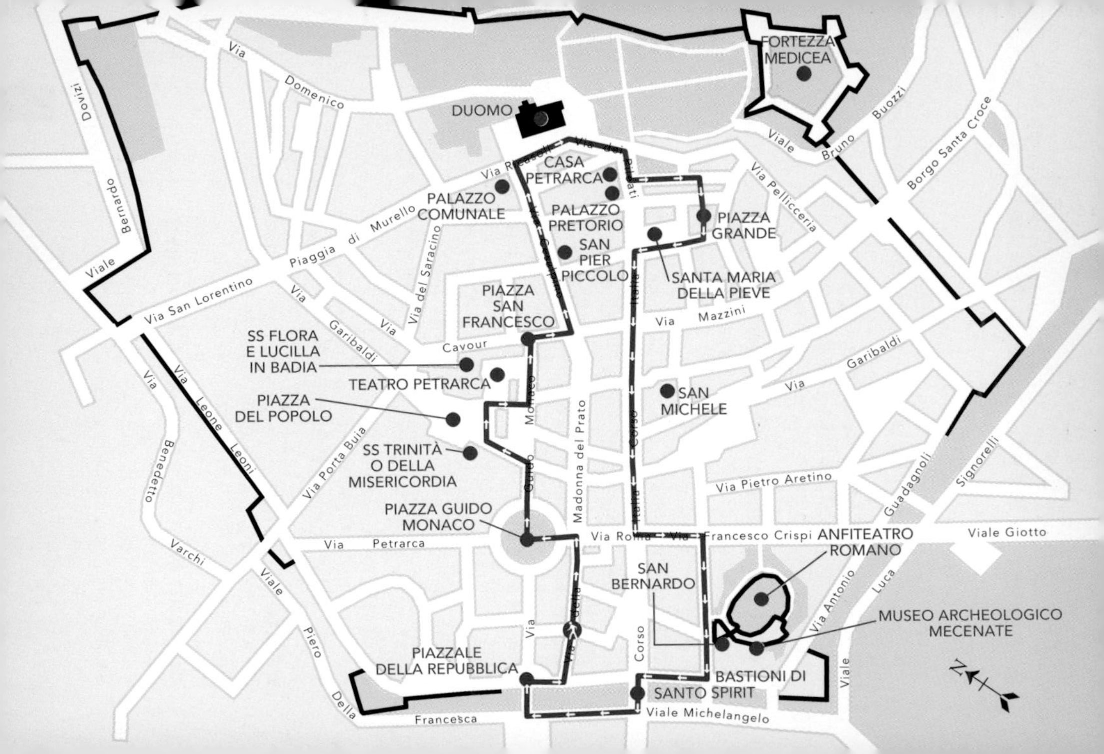

FORTEZZA MEDICEA
DUOMO
CASA PETRARCA
PALAZZO COMUNALE
PALAZZO PRETORIO
SAN PIER PICCOLO
PIAZZA GRANDE
SANTA MARIA DELLA PIEVE
PIAZZA SAN FRANCESCO
SS FLORA E LUCILLA IN BADIA
TEATRO PETRARCA
PIAZZA DEL POPOLO
SS TRINITÀ O DELLA MISERICORDIA
SAN MICHELE
PIAZZA GUIDO MONACO
ANFITEATRO ROMANO
SAN BERNARDO
MUSEO ARCHEOLOGICO MECENATE
BASTIONI DI SANTO SPIRIT
PIAZZALE DELLA REPUBBLICA
Via Domenico
Viale Bernardo Dovizi
Via Ricasoli
Via dei Pileati
Piaggia di Murello
Via del Saracino
Via San Lorentino
Via Garibaldi
Via Cavour
Via Cesalpino
Via Guido Monaco
Madonna del Prato
Corso Italia
Via Mazzini
Via Pellicceria
Viale Bruno Buozzi
Borgo Santa Croce
Via Garibaldi
Via Pietro Aretino
Guadagnoli
Signorelli
Viale Giotto
Via Roma
Via Francesco Crispi
Via Petrarca
Via Leone Leoni
Via Benedetto Varchi
Via Porta Buia
Viale Piero Della Francesca
Via della
Corso
Viale Michelangelo
Via Antonio
Viale Luca
Z

Duration: 3 hr.
Start from the tourist office at Piazza Risorgimento 116, turn left into Via della Madonna del Prato, past two *trattorie,* and left again along the main Via Roma to the large tree-lined Piazza Guido Monaco where the excellent Hotel-Restaurant Continentale (see **AREZZO-RESTAURANTS**) is on the corner. Turn right on Via Guido Monaco and half-left past the church of SS Trinità o della Misericordia into Piazza del Popolo. Ahead are the Basilica SS Flora e Lucilla in Badia and the Teatro Petrarca. Turn right past the Poste e Telegrafi to Via Guido Monaco and left into the restored Piazza San Francesco with its famous church (see **AREZZO-ATTRACTIONS**). Stop a while to admire Piero della Francesca's (see **A-Z**) frescoes, *The Legend of the True Cross,* a strange saga of battles, archangels, Solomon and the Queen of Sheba, and the emperor Constantine. Follow Via Cesalpino and on the right after 100 m is the church of San Pier Piccolo. Another 100 m further on is the handsome Palazzo Comunale (town hall), with dozens of carved badges and escutcheons on the outer walls. The imposing Duomo (see **AREZZO-ATTRACTIONS**) lies in front. There are fine works inside by the Frenchman Marcillat, a fresco of Mary Magdalene by Piero della Francesca and 16thC marble pulpits. Behind the Duomo on the top of the hill are woods (Passeggio del Prato) and ramparts. From here there are superb views, making this a good place for a picnic. To the right (200 m southeast) is the 16thC Fortezza Medicea (0900-1900; free), from where there are views to the Apennines. The pentagon-shaped, battlemented fortress now has peaceful gardens and cypress trees. Turn half-right on Via dei Pileati past Casa Petrarca, where Petrarch, the great romantic poet, was born, Palazzo Pretorio, the musical academy, and downhill into the *centro storico,* which fortunately escaped damage in World War II, to the main sight of Arezzo, the famous fan-shaped Piazza Grande (see **AREZZO-ATTRACTIONS**). It is surrounded by medieval houses, towers, arcades, a splendid *tribunale* (law courts) and Vasari's (see **A-Z**) long loggia. In Sep. the unusual Saracen's Tournament takes place here, when four teams of horsemen tilt and charge a large revolving 'Saracen' figure (which fights back!). Leave at the southwest corner to see the Chiesa di Santa Maria della Pieve (see **AREZZO-ATTRACTIONS**) with its superb campanile, Pisan Romanesque

OROLOGERIA
BURZI
LORENZ

façade, and inside a polyptych (panelled altarpiece) by Pietro Lorenzetti (see **A-Z**). Turn left, downhill on the long, flagstoned Corso Italia past the church of San Michele, a number of *palazzi*, restaurants and small boutiques to Via Roma again. Turn left for 100 m then turn right into Via Margaritone. Towards the end is the little church of San Bernardo, the Museo Archeologico Mecenate (see **AREZZO-ATTRACTIONS**) at No. 10 and the Roman amphitheatre (Anfiteatro Romano). The railway station is 250 m on the right past the Bastioni di Santo Spirito, while Piazzale della Repubblica and the tourist office are a further 100 m northeast.

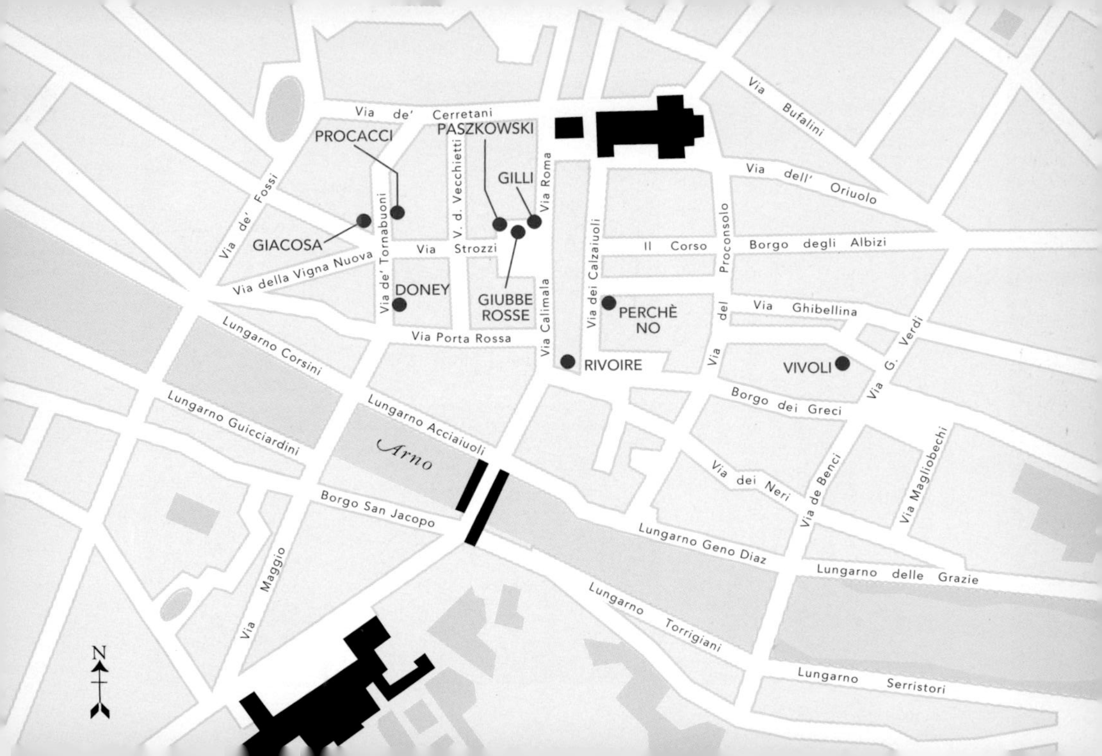
Via de' Cerretani
PROCACCI
PASZKOWSKI
GILLI
Via Roma
Via Bufalini
Via dell' Oriuolo
Via de' Fossi
GIACOSA
Via de' Tornabuoni
V. d. Vecchietti
Via Strozzi
Il Corso
Proconsolo
Borgo degli Albizi
Via della Vigna Nuova
DONEY
GIUBBE ROSSE
Via Calimala
Via dei Calzaiuoli
PERCHÈ NO
Via del
Via Ghibellina
Via Porta Rossa
RIVOIRE
VIVOLI
Via G. Verdi
Lungarno Corsini
Borgo dei Greci
Lungarno Guicciardini
Lungarno Acciaiuoli
Arno
Via dei Neri
Via de Benci
Via Magliobechi
Borgo San Jacopo
Lungarno Geno Diaz
Lungarno delle Grazie
Via Maggio
Lungarno Torrigiani
Lungarno Serristori
N

DONEY Piazza Strozzi 16-19. ■ 0800-2045 Wed.-Mon.
A literary rendezvous in the 19thC. Still an elegant café-restaurant today; tea is served on the floral terrace outside.

GIACOSA Via Tornabuoni 83r-87r.
■ 0730-2030 Mon.-Sun.
Handmade chocolates, marrons glacés *and the best cappuccino in town.*

PERCHÈ NO Via Tavolini 19r.
■ 0800-2400 Wed.-Mon.
Has 30 exclusive varieties of terrific ice cream, sorbets and semi-freddo.

RIVOIRE Piazza della Signoria 5r. ■ 0800-0030 Tue.-Sun.
Serves superb hot chocolate but it's rather expensive as you'll have to pay for the views of the Palazzo Vecchio (see **FLORENCE-PALAZZI***). Situated in a handsome grey* palazzo *with a large outdoor terrace.*

VIVOLI Via dell Isola delle Stinche 7. ■ 0800-0100 Tue.-Sun. am.
Modest premises but one of the best gelateria *in Tuscany. Note the plaque commemorating local hero Giovanni Dupré who lived here.*

PASZKOWSKI Piazza della Repubblica 6r.
■ 0730-0100 Tue.-Sun.
Open-air café where a band called Caffe Concerto plays each evening.

GILLI Piazza della Repubblica 39r. ■ 0800-2400 Wed.-Mon.
A stylish belle époque *café with music on summer evenings and a huge outdoor terrace.*

GIUBBE ROSSE Piazza della Repubblica. ■ 0800-2400 Wed.-Mon.
Literary café-restaurant with alfresco ices and snacks. There's also a tearoom serving 'English tea' and 'American breakfast'.

PROCACCI Via Tornabuoni 64.
■ 0800-1300 Mon.-Sat., 1630-1945 Mon., Tue. & Thu.-Sat.
In a sophisticated setting; serves super truffle rolls.

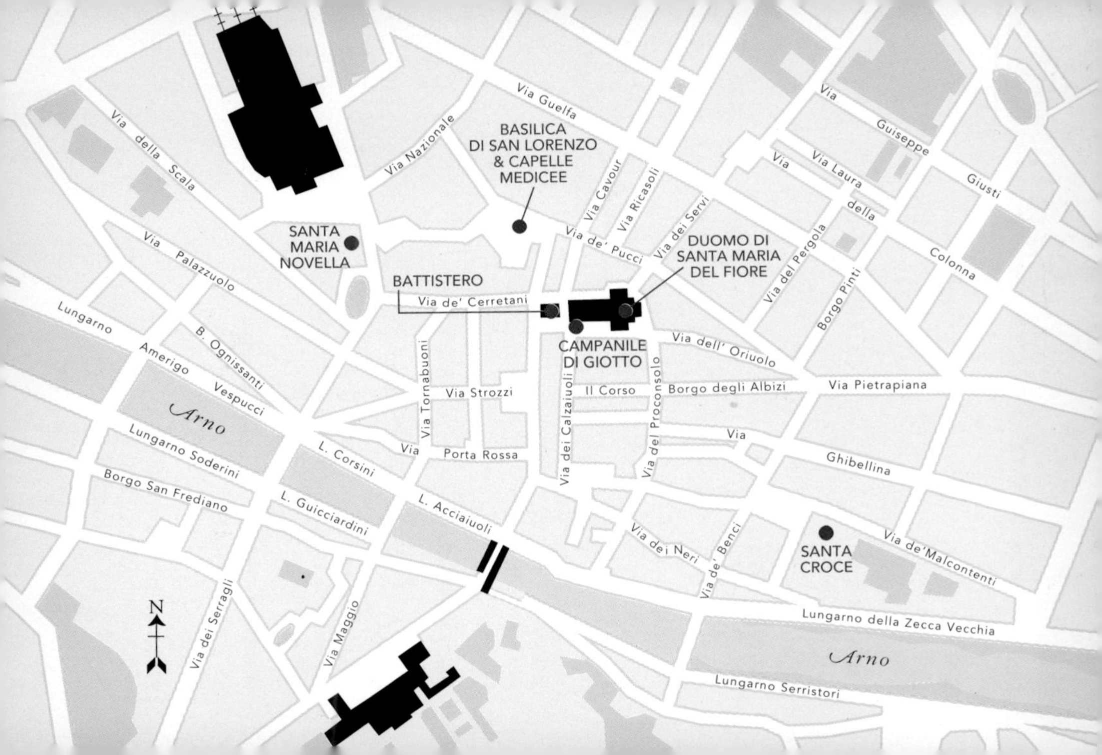
Via della Scala
Via Nazionale
Via Guelfa
BASILICA DI SAN LORENZO & CAPELLE MEDICEE
Via Giuseppe Giusti
Via Laura
Via della Colonna
SANTA MARIA NOVELLA
Via Palazzuolo
Via Cavour
Via Ricasoli
Via de' Pucci
Via dei Servi
DUOMO DI SANTA MARIA DEL FIORE
Via del Pergola
Borgo Pinti
BATTISTERO
Via de' Cerretani
Lungarno Amerigo Vespucci
B. Ognissanti
CAMPANILE DI GIOTTO
Via dell' Oriuolo
Via Tornabuoni
Via Strozzi
Via dei Calzaiuoli
Il Corso
Via del Proconsolo
Borgo degli Albizi
Via Pietrapiana
Arno
Lungarno Soderini
L. Corsini
Via Porta Rossa
Via Ghibellina
Borgo San Frediano
L. Guicciardini
L. Acciaiuoli
Via dei Neri
Via de' Benci
SANTA CROCE
Via de'Malcontenti
N
Via dei Serragli
Via Maggio
Lungarno della Zecca Vecchia
Arno
Lungarno Serristori

DUOMO DI SANTA MARIA DEL FIORE Piazza del Duomo.
■ Duomo 0700-1700; Crypt & lantern dome 1030-1700.
● Duomo Free; Crypt L.5000; Lantern dome L.6000.
Magnificent 13thC cathedral with marble mosaic façade in white, green and pink. Note Brunelleschi's dome and the crypt of Santa Reparata.

CAMPANILE DI GIOTTO Next to Duomo.
■ 0900-1900 summer, 0900-1700 winter. ● L.6000.
Climb 414 steps up the tower for superb views. Note works by Pisano and della Robbia. Giotto was responsible for the general design in 1334.

BATTISTERO 50 m west of Duomo.
■ 0900-1230, 1430-1730. ● Free.
Green and white marble clads Florence's oldest building, built in the 7th-11thC and octagonal in shape. Study Pisano (see **A-Z***) and Ghiberti's (see* **A-Z***) bronze doors –* Porta del Paradiso *– and 13thC mosaics.*

SANTA CROCE Piazza Santa Croce.
■ 0700-1230, 1500-1830. ● Free.
13th-14thC Franciscan church. Has frescoes by Giotto and Gaddi, Donatello's Crucifix *and* Annunciation*, and the tombs of Michelangelo, Dante, Galileo, Rossini and Machiavelli.* *See* **FLORENCE-MUSEUMS 2**.

BASILICA DI SAN LORENZO & CAPELLE MEDICEE
Piazza San Lorenzo/Piazza Madonna. ■ Basilica 0700-1215, 1530-1730; Chapels 0900-1400 Tue.-Sun. ● Basilica Free; Chapels L.11,000.
In the 15th-17thC the Medici (see **A-Z***) commissioned Brunelleschi, Donatello and Lippi to build this monumental complex, including the Laurentian library and Medici chapels, to house their tombs. There are marvellous sculptures, drawings, sketches and frescoes by Michelangelo.*

SANTA MARIA NOVELLA Piazza Santa Maria Novella.
■ Main complex 0700-1130, 1530-1800; Cloisters 0900-1400 Sat.-Thu. ● Main complex Free; Cloisters L.6000.
13th-15thC Dominican complex with sacristy, chapels, refectory and cloisters, housing works by Lippi, Masaccio, Ghirlandaio and Vasari.

SANTISSIMA ANNUNZIATA
BADIA FIORENTINA
ORSANMICHELE
SANTA TRINITÀ
SANTO SPIRITO
SANTA MARIA DEL CARMINE
SAN MINIATO AL MONTE
N
Arno
Arno
Via Guelfa
Via Nazionale
Via della Scala
Via Palazzuolo
Lungarno Amerigo Vespucci
B. Ognissanti
Lungarno Soderini
Borgo San Frediano
Via dei Serragli
Via Maggio
L. Guicciardini
L. Corsini
L. Acciaiuoli
Via Porta Rossa
Via Tornabuoni
Via Strozzi
Via de' Cerretani
Via Cavour
Via Ricasoli
Via de' Pucci
Via dei Servi
Via Laura
Via della Pergola
Via Guiseppe Giusti
Via della Colonna
Borgo Pinti
Via dell' Oriuolo
Il Corso
Borgo degli Albizi
Via Pietrapiana
Via dei Calzaiuoli
Via del Proconsolo
Via Ghibellina
Via dei Neri
Via de' Benci
Via de'Malcontenti
Lungarno della Zecca Vecchia
Lungarno Serristori

SAN MINIATO AL MONTE Mte alle Croci, Viale Galileo Galilei.
■ 0800-1200, 1400-1900. Bus 13.
After the Battistero the oldest church in Florence (1090). It has a 13thC mosaic, the Cardinal of Portugal's chapel, terracotta works by della Robbia, a sacristy with frescoes by Aretino and a marble pulpit (1209).

SANTO SPIRITO Piazza Santo Spirito.
■ 0800-1200, 1600-1800.
Brunelleschi's mid-15thC design with a bell tower has 40 semicircular chapels, an octagonal sacristy, Lippi altarpiece and vaulted vestibule.

SANTA TRINITÀ Piazza Santa Trinità.
■ 0700-1200, 1600-1900.
Gothic interior and baroque façade. Note the Ghirlandaio frescoes, della Robbia's tomb of Bishop Federighi and the Sassetti sarcophagi.

SANTA MARIA DEL CARMINE Piazza del Carmine.
■ 0900-1200, 1530-1830.
A 13th-15thC church with Masaccio frescoes, and the Brancacci and Corsini chapels. A fire in 1771 destroyed much but spared the chapels.

ORSANMICHELE Via dei Calzaiuoli.
■ 0800-1200, 1530-1830.
Originally a grain market, from 1380 it was used as an oratory. See Orcagna's tabernacle and Verrocchio, Donatello and Ghiberti sculptures.

SANTISSIMA ANNUNZIATA Piazza della Santissima Annunziata.
■ 0700-1230, 1600-1900.
Founded in 1234, this Renaissance church has a gilded nave, del Sarto frescoes, Michelozzo's Miraculous Image of the Virgin *and Feroni chapel.*

BADIA FIORENTINA Via del Proconsolo.
■ 0800-1200, 1630-1830.
Dante (see **A-Z***) saw Beatrice at Mass in this Benedictine abbey, founded in* AD *978. Note the hexagonal Romanesque campanile, Lippi's* St. Bernard's Vision of the Madonna *and Rossellino's 15thC cloisters.*

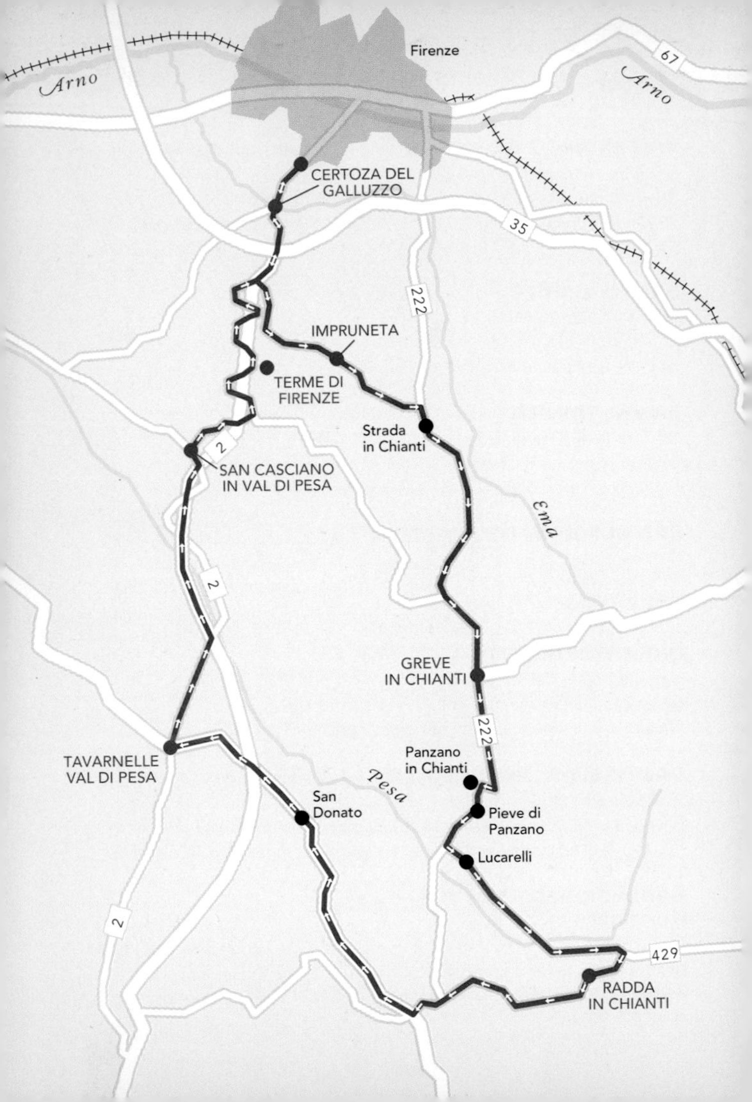

Firenze
Arno
67
Arno
CERTOZA DEL GALLUZZO
35
222
IMPRUNETA
TERME DI FIRENZE
Strada in Chianti
2
SAN CASCIANO IN VAL DI PESA
Ema
2
GREVE IN CHIANTI
222
Panzano in Chianti
TAVARNELLE VAL DI PESA
Pesa
San Donato
Pieve di Panzano
Lucarelli
2
429
RADDA IN CHIANTI

A half-day excursion south to the Chianti wine-growing area.

Cross the river Arno (see **A-Z**) by the Ponte alla Carraia and Via de' Serragli to the large Piazza della Porta Romana. The Via Senese (SS 2) is signposted Siena and Rome. After 5 km stop to see the Certosa del Galluzzo (0900-1200, 1600-1900; L.6000), a Carthusian monastery of 1341 with frescoes by Pontormo, paintings by Cranach and Bronzino Il and 64 della Robbia (see **A-Z**) terracotta heads. The monks' liqueurs and honey are on sale. Keep on the SS 2 and pass under the autostrada. Shortly afterwards take a minor road to the left and southeast for 7 km.
16 km – Impruneta. The 11thC Basilica di Santa Maria all'Impruneta (1054) is worth a look and the local artisans produce attractive terracotta giftware. You are now entering the chianti gallo nero wine-growing area, a large oval-shaped region halfway between Florence and Siena. Blue signs indicate wine growers whose wines you can taste and buy. Go southeast for 6 km to join the SS 222 (the 18thC wine road called the Strada Chiantigiana) through Strada in Chianti. Continue for 11 km.
33 km – Greve in Chianti. This is the capital of the gallo nero (black cockerel) classico region, a small charming town with a triangular market square, convent (1400), the battered castle of Mte Fioralle, a dozen restaurants and a major wine fair (see **A-Z**). Advice on estates to visit and tasting facilities can be obtained at the Enoteca del Chianti Classico. Continue south on the SS 222 through Panzano in Chianti, Pieve di Panzano and Lucarelli.
59 km – Radda in Chianti. A small fortified hill town. The 14thC *palazzo*, once a medieval fortress, is now the town hall with a small Etruscan museum (0900-1230, 1500-1830 Wed.-Sat., 0930-1230 Sun.; L.5000); three Etruscan tombs can be seen nearby at Mte Calvario. The town overlooks three river valleys and the churches, castle and *palazzi* are hidden behind grape silos. The Bottega del Chianti Classico is the wine-tasting centre. Take a minor road northwest for 10 km to San Donato, then another 8 km to Tavarnelle Val di Pesa on the SS 2. The road forms the western boundary of the classico wine region. On the return journey is San Casciano in Val di Pesa, with medieval town walls and five notable churches. Continue through Terme di Firenze, a small spa, and return to Florence by your original route.

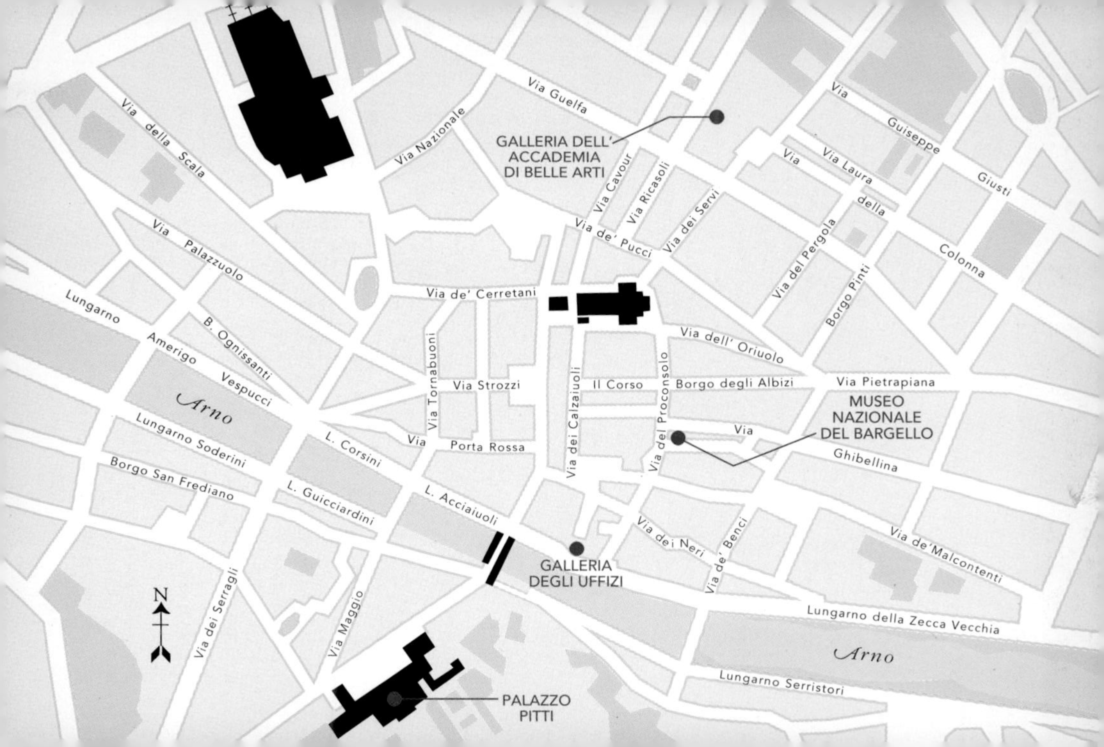
GALLERIA DELL' ACCADEMIA DI BELLE ARTI
MUSEO NAZIONALE DEL BARGELLO
GALLERIA DEGLI UFFIZI
PALAZZO PITTI
Via della Scala
Via Nazionale
Via Guelfa
Via Giuseppe Giusti
Via Laura
Via della Colonna
Via Cavour
Via Ricasoli
Via dei Servi
Via de' Pucci
Via del Pergola
Borgo Pinti
Via Palazzuolo
B. Ognissanti
Lungarno Amerigo Vespucci
Via de' Cerretani
Via dell' Oriuolo
Via Tornabuoni
Via Strozzi
Via dei Calzaiuoli
Il Corso
Via del Proconsolo
Borgo degli Albizi
Via Pietrapiana
Via Ghibellina
Via Porta Rossa
Arno
Lungarno Soderini
L. Corsini
Borgo San Frediano
L. Guicciardini
L. Acciaiuoli
Via dei Neri
Via de' Benci
Via de'Malcontenti
Lungarno della Zecca Vecchia
Lungarno Serristori
Via dei Serragli
Via Maggio
N

GALLERIA DEGLI UFFIZI Loggiato degli Uffizi 6.
0900-1900 Tue.-Sat., 0900-1300 Sun. L.11,000.
Vasari's (see **A-Z***) building (1560) for Cosimo I's offices holds 1700 superb works of art in 45 rooms. The 15thC Renaissance School of Florentine paintings is in rooms 7 and 8, and the Medici Botticellis in 10-14. Works by Leonardo da Vinci (room 15), Michelangelo (25), Raphael (26), Titian (28), Veronese (34), Rubens (41) and Rembrandt (44) should also be seen. Allow several hours to digest!*

GALLERIA DELL'ACCADEMIA DI BELLE ARTI Via Ricasoli.
0900-1400 Tue.-Sun. L.11,000.
Founded in 1784, the original Academy of Art contains important works by Michelangelo (see **A-Z***), including his famous* David *and* Four Slaves, *and* Madonna of the Sea *by Botticelli (see* **A-Z***).*

PALAZZO PITTI Piazza Pitti.
0900-1400 Tue.-Sun., 0900-1300 Sun. Palatine Gallery L.9000; Silver L.7000; Modern Art L.5000; Costume L.7000.
Brunelleschi designed this huge Renaissance building, in which Maria de' Medici lived, and also the grand dukes from 1550 onwards. Today it houses eight museums. The Palatine Gallery has Titians, Raphaels, Rubens and Van Dycks; the Royal Apartments on the 1st floor contain furnishings, Medici portraits and tapestries; and the Silver Museum on the ground floor has Medici treasures and frescoes. In addition, there are the Gallery of Modern Art on the 2nd floor and the Contini-Bonacossi collection with nearly 150 objets d'art. *The Porcelain Museum is in the Casino del Cavaliere; the Costume Museum in the Palazzina della Meridiana; and there's also the Museum of Carriages. Usually at least two museums are closed for restoration.* *See* **FLORENCE-PALAZZI**.

MUSEO NAZIONALE DEL BARGELLO Via del Proconsolo 4.
0900-1400 Tue.-Sat., 0900-1300 Sun. & hols. L.7000.
This 13th-14thC palace with its splendid courtyard has Michelangelo (see **A-Z***) sculptures, including the original bronze* David, *and works by Donatello, as well as della Robbia terracottas and Verrocchio's* David. *The* bargello *was the medieval constable and chief magistrate.*

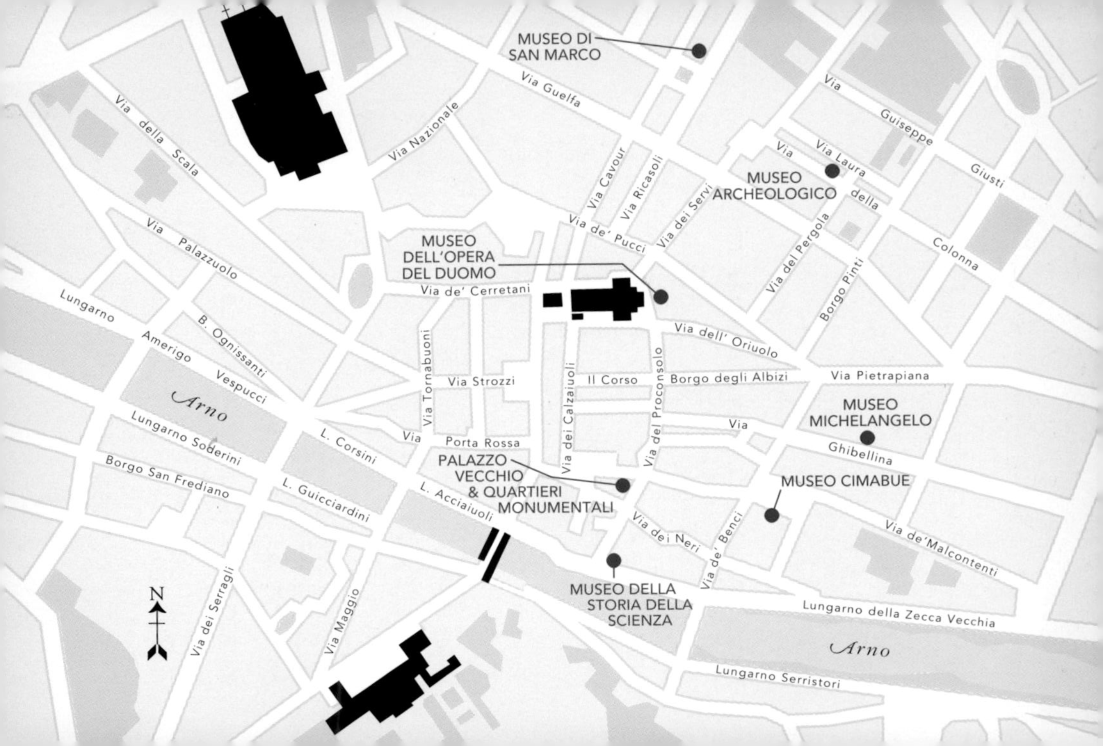
MUSEO DI SAN MARCO
MUSEO ARCHEOLOGICO
MUSEO DELL'OPERA DEL DUOMO
MUSEO MICHELANGELO
MUSEO CIMABUE
PALAZZO VECCHIO & QUARTIERI MONUMENTALI
MUSEO DELLA STORIA DELLA SCIENZA
Via Guelfa
Via Nazionale
Via della Scala
Via Palazzuolo
Via Cavour
Via Ricasoli
Via dei Servi
Via de' Pucci
Via Laura
Via Giuseppe Giusti
Via della Colonna
Via del Pergola
Borgo Pinti
Via de' Cerretani
Via dell' Oriuolo
Via Tornabuoni
Via Strozzi
Via dei Calzaiuoli
Il Corso
Via del Proconsolo
Borgo degli Albizi
Via Pietrapiana
Via Ghibellina
Via Porta Rossa
Via dei Neri
Via de' Benci
Via de'Malcontenti
Lungarno della Zecca Vecchia
Lungarno Serristori
Lungarno Amerigo Vespucci
B. Ognissanti
Lungarno Soderini
Borgo San Frediano
L. Corsini
L. Guicciardini
L. Acciaiuoli
Via dei Serragli
Via Maggio
Arno
Arno
N

MUSEO DI SAN MARCO Piazza San Marco.
0900-1400 Tue.-Sat., 0900-1300 Sun. & hols. L.7000.
Fra Angelico's frescoes and paintings are in the convent and cloister of Sant'Antonino, the Sala Capitolare and Ospizio dei Pellegrini. On the 1st floor are 44 dormitory cells and Fra Angelico's Annunciation *fresco.*

MUSEO DELL'OPERA DEL DUOMO Piazza del Duomo 9.
0900-1400 Mon.-Sat., 0900-1300 Sun. L.6000, Free Sun.
Houses sacred art from the Duomo, Battistero and Campanile (see **FLORENCE-CHURCHES 1***), including works by Pisano and Donatello.*

MUSEO CIMABUE Piazza Santa Croce 16.
1000-1230, 1530-1830 Thu.-Tue. L.5000.
In the monastery refectory are Cimabue's Crucifixion*, Gaddi's* The Last Supper *and Donatello's* St. Louis of Toulouse. *See* **FLORENCE-CHURCHES 1**.

PALAZZO VECCHIO & QUARTIERI MONUMENTALI
Piazza della Signoria.
0900-1900 Mon.-Fri., 0800-1300 Sun. L.7000, Free Sun.
The State apartments house Cronaca's Salone dei Cinquecento*, Michel-angelo's* Genius of Victory *and Bronzino frescoes. See* **FLORENCE-PALAZZI**.

MUSEO MICHELANGELO (CASA BUONARROTI)
Via Ghibellina 70. 0930-1330 Wed.-Mon. L.7000.
Michelangelo's great-nephew built this museum and assembled his great-uncle's works, including working drawings and early sculptures. See the Madonna della Scala *(1490-92) and a wooden crucifix.*

MUSEO ARCHEOLOGICO Via della Colonna 36.
0900-1400 Tue.-Sun. L.8000.
Etruscan, Egyptian, Greek and Roman collections in a 17thC palazzo.

MUSEO DELLA STORIA DELLA SCIENZA Piazza dei Giudici.
0930-1300 Mon.-Sat., 1400-1700 Mon., Wed. & Fri. L.7000.
In the medieval Palazzo Castellani. See the alchemist's laboratory, giant armillary sphere of 1593, Galileo's telescope and the great lodestone.

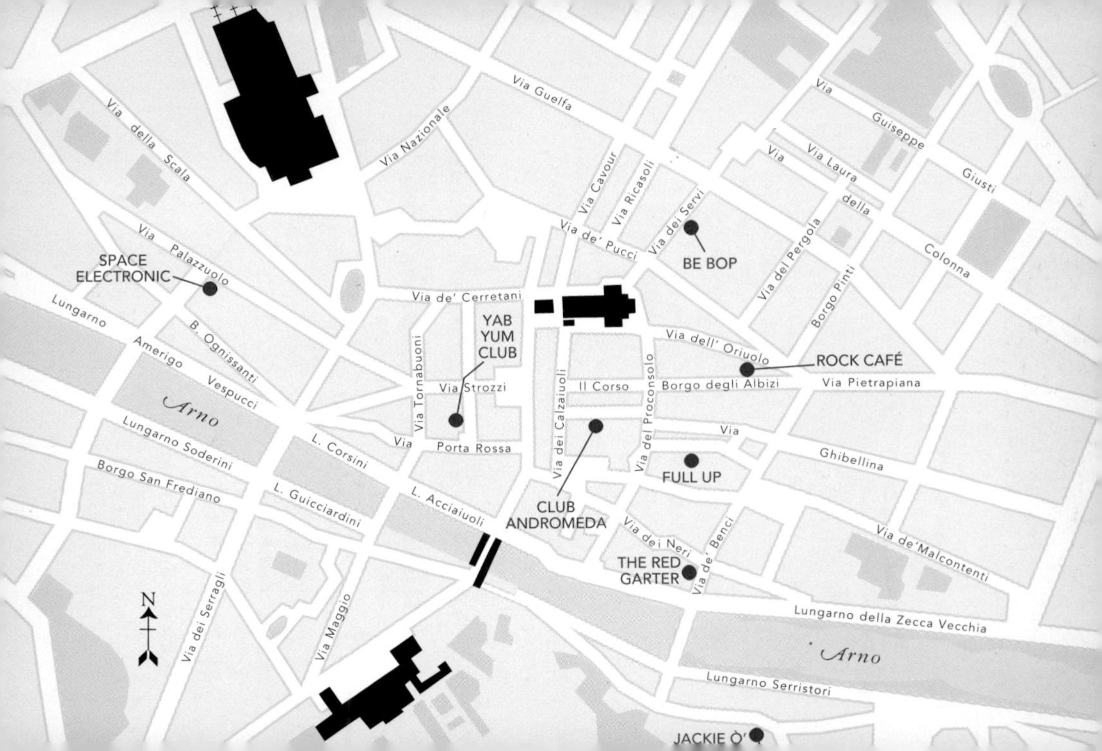

SPACE ELECTRONIC
YAB YUM CLUB
BE BOP
ROCK CAFÉ
CLUB ANDROMEDA
FULL UP
THE RED GARTER
JACKIE Ò'
Via della Scala
Via Nazionale
Via Guelfa
Via Guiseppe Giusti
Via Laura
Via della Colonna
Via Cavour
Via Ricasoli
Via dei Servi
Via de' Pucci
Via del Pergola
Borgo Pinti
Via Palazzuolo
Lungarno Amerigo Vespucci
B. Ognissanti
Via de' Cerretani
Via Tornabuoni
Via Strozzi
Via Porta Rossa
Via dei Calzaiuoli
Il Corso
Via del Proconsolo
Via dell' Oriuolo
Borgo degli Albizi
Via Pietrapiana
Via Ghibellina
Arno
Lungarno Soderini
Borgo San Frediano
L. Corsini
L. Guicciardini
L. Acciaiuoli
Via dei Neri
Via de' Benci
Via de'Malcontenti
Lungarno della Zecca Vecchia
Lungarno Serristori
Via dei Serragli
Via Maggio
N

YAB YUM CLUB Via dei Sassetti 5r.
■ 2200-0430 Tue. & Thu.-Sun. ● L.25,000 inc. first drink.
A smart, sophisticated disco which is popular with young Florentines. In summer it moves to the Parco delle Cascine.

SPACE ELECTRONIC Via Palazzuolo 37.
■ 2100-0300. Closed Mon. in winter. ● L.20,000 inc. first drink.
The largest and most popular disco in town with great rock music, two dance floors and videos, set incongruously in a grand palazzo*!*

BE BOP Via dei Servi 76r.
■ 2000-0330 Mon.-Sat. Closed Aug. ● L.25,000 inc. first drink.
The best live jazz, folk, blues and country music in Florence.

JACKIE Ò' Via dell'Erta Canina 42b.
■ 2200-0300 Mon.-Sat. ● L.30,000 inc. first drink. Premium charge Fri. & Sat.
An excellent large disco and piano bar, with all the latest sounds.

FULL UP Via della Vigna Vecchia 21r.
■ 2200-0300 Wed.-Mon. Closed Aug. ● L.25,000 inc. first drink.
Crowded, fashionable disco and piano bar with interesting décor.

ROCK CAFÉ Borgo degli Albizi 66.
■ 2200-0300 Wed.-Mon. Closed Aug. ● L.25,000 inc. first drink.
A piano bar and disco which also hosts rock concerts.

CLUB ANDROMEDA Via dei Cimatori 13r.
■ 2200-0300 Tue.-Sun. Closed Aug. ● L.25,000 inc. first drink.
A disco with two dance floors and great laser effects. There is an excellent floor show every Sun.

THE RED GARTER Via de' Benci 33r.
■ 2030-0130. ● L.12,000 inc. first drink.
Has rock bands and sometimes an American banjo band; noisy but inexpensive. It claims to be the *American nightclub.*

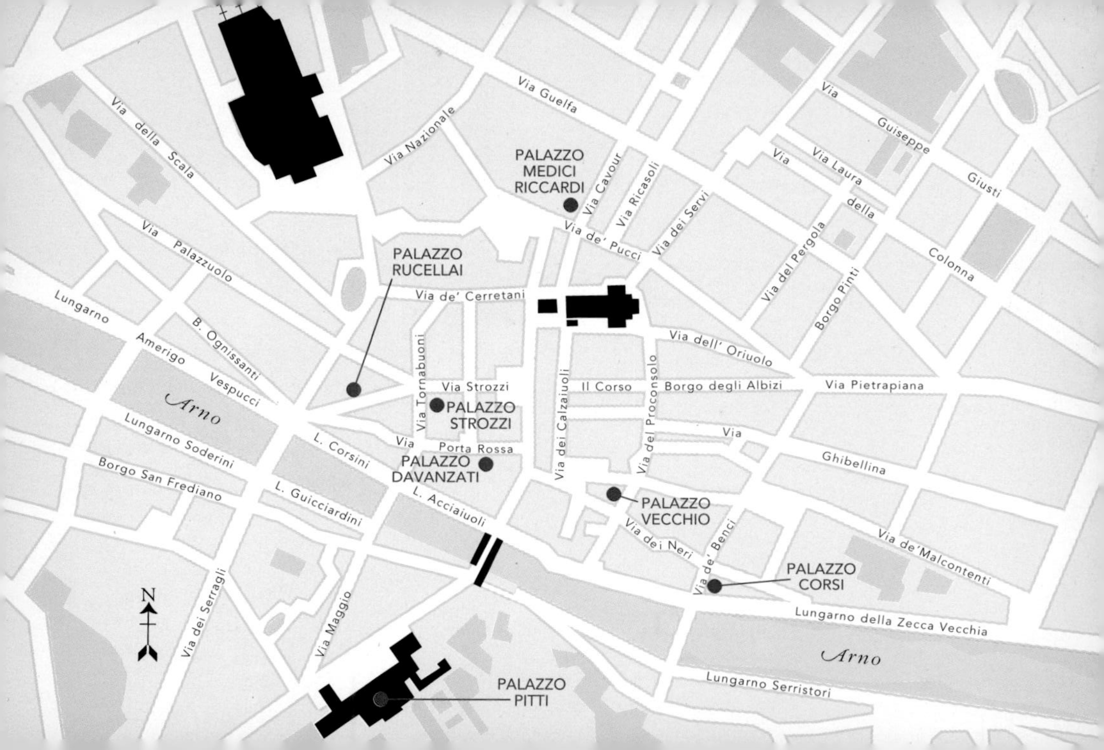

PALAZZO MEDICI RICCARDI
PALAZZO RUCELLAI
PALAZZO STROZZI
PALAZZO DAVANZATI
PALAZZO VECCHIO
PALAZZO CORSI
PALAZZO PITTI
Arno
Arno
N
Via della Scala
Via Nazionale
Via Guelfa
Via Cavour
Via Ricasoli
Via dei Servi
Via de' Pucci
Via Giuseppe Giusti
Via
Via Laura
Via della Colonna
Via del Pergola
Borgo Pinti
Via Palazzuolo
Via de' Cerretani
Lungarno Amerigo Vespucci
B. Ognissanti
Via dell' Oriuolo
Via Tornabuoni
Via Strozzi
Il Corso
Borgo degli Albizi
Via Pietrapiana
Via dei Calzaiuoli
Via del Proconsolo
Via
Ghibellina
Via Porta Rossa
L. Corsini
Lungarno Soderini
Borgo San Frediano
L. Guicciardini
L. Acciaiuoli
Via dei Neri
Via de' Benci
Via de' Malcontenti
Lungarno della Zecca Vecchia
Lungarno Serristori
Via dei Serragli
Via Maggio

PALAZZO VECCHIO (PALAZZO DELLA SIGNORIA)
Piazza della Signoria.
■ 0900-1900 Mon.-Fri., 0900-1300 Sun. ● L.9000.
*Powerful 13thC building owned by the guilds, magnates (*signoria*) and Medici. Note the 94 m-high watchtower. See* **FLORENCE-MUSEUMS 2**.

PALAZZO STROZZI Via Tornabuoni.
■ 1600-1900 Mon., Wed. & Fri. ● Free.
Filippo Strozzi built this huge palace in 1489-1536. Note Grosso's fine lamp brackets and the elegant courtyard loggia in the Museo Piccolo.

PALAZZO DAVANZATI Piazza Davanzati/Via Porta Rossa 13.
■ 0900-1400 Tue.-Sat. ● L.6000.
The best-preserved 14thC Florentine palazzo*, complete with courtyard, staircase, well, kitchens, wall decorations and medieval lavatories!*

PALAZZO MEDICI RICCARDI Via Cavour 1. ■ 0900-1230, 1500-1700 Mon., Tue. & Thu.-Sat., 0900-1200 Sun. ● Free.
Designed in the 15thC by Michelozzo for the Medici (see **A-Z***). The Medici museum has a Lippi altarpiece, and the chapel Gozzoli frescoes.*

PALAZZO RUCELLAI Via della Vigna Nuova 18.
■ Open by request only. Ask at the tourist office for details.
The most beautiful of all Florentine palaces, built in 1450 for Giovanni Rucellai by Rossellino to Alberti's design.

PALAZZO PITTI Piazza de' Pitti.
The yellow façade, 200 m long, was built by Brunelleschi (see **A-Z***) in 1440 for the wealthy merchant Luca Pitti. In 1550 the Medici (see* **A-Z***) purchased the palace and moved in. In 1555 Vasari's (see* **A-Z***)* corridoio *was built across the river to the 'old' Palazzo Vecchio. See* **FLORENCE-MUSEUMS 1**.

PALAZZO CORSI Via de' Benci.
■ 0900-1300 Mon.-Sat. ● L.5000.
Built in 1489 for the wealthy Corsi cloth merchant family, it now houses Herbert Percy Horne's museum, with Daddi, Lorenzetti and Lippi works.

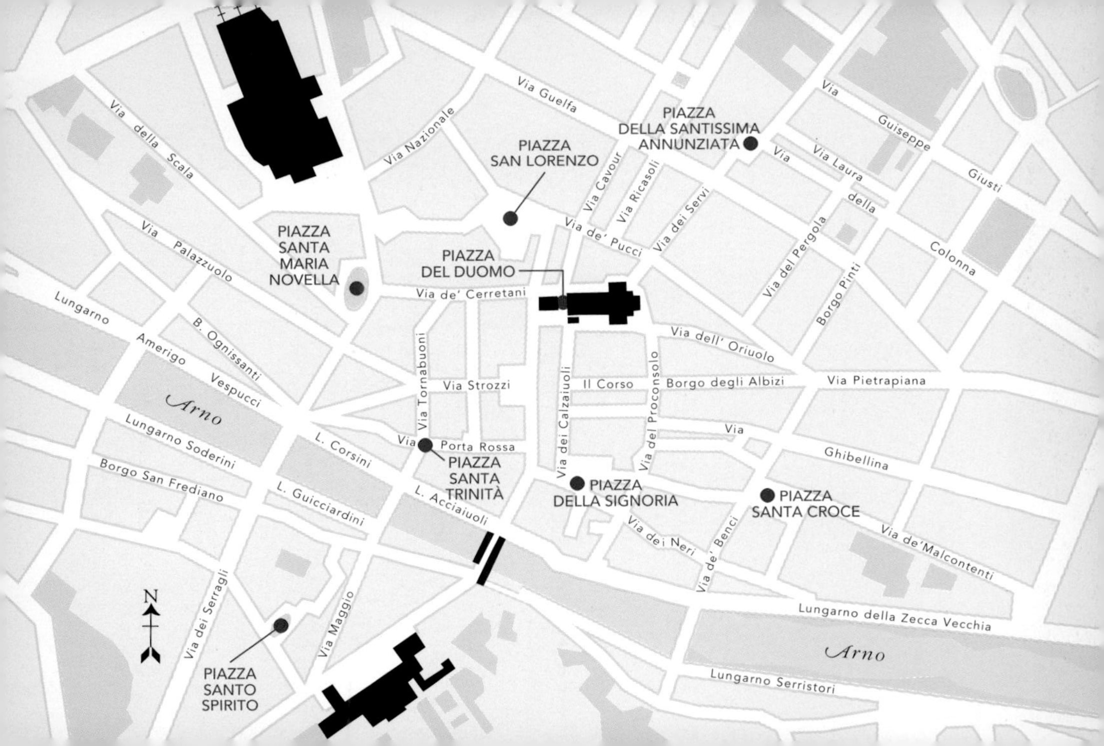
PIAZZA DELLA SANTISSIMA ANNUNZIATA
PIAZZA SAN LORENZO
PIAZZA SANTA MARIA NOVELLA
PIAZZA DEL DUOMO
PIAZZA SANTA TRINITÀ
PIAZZA DELLA SIGNORIA
PIAZZA SANTA CROCE
PIAZZA SANTO SPIRITO
Via della Scala
Via Nazionale
Via Guelfa
Via Guiseppe Giusti
Via Laura
Via della Colonna
Via Cavour
Via Ricasoli
Via dei Servi
Via de' Pucci
Via del Pergola
Borgo Pinti
Via Palazzuolo
Via de' Cerretani
Lungarno Amerigo Vespucci
B. Ognissanti
Via dell' Oriuolo
Via Tornabuoni
Via Strozzi
Via dei Calzaiuoli
Il Corso
Via del Proconsolo
Borgo degli Albizi
Via Pietrapiana
Arno
Lungarno Soderini
L. Corsini
Via Porta Rossa
Via Ghibellina
Borgo San Frediano
L. Guicciardini
L. Acciaiuoli
Via dei Neri
Via de' Benci
Via de'Malcontenti
Lungarno della Zecca Vecchia
Arno
Lungarno Serristori
Via dei Serragli
Via Maggio
N

PIAZZA DEL DUOMO
The splendour of the Duomo, the octagonal elegance of the Battistero and the grace of the Campanile (see **FLORENCE-CHURCHES 1***) make this the most beautiful square in Florence. See* **FLORENCE-WALK**.

PIAZZA DELLA SIGNORIA
The historical and political heart of the city, dominated by the Palazzo Vecchio (see **FLORENCE-PALAZZI***). Savonarola (see* **A-Z***) was executed here. See* **FLORENCE-WALK**.

PIAZZA DELLA SANTISSIMA ANNUNZIATA
A beautifully proportioned square bordered by elegant porticoes and the 16thC Palazzo Riccardi-Mannelli. There are two bronze fountains (1629) and an equestrian statue of Grand Duke Ferdinando I.

PIAZZA SANTA TRINITÀ
A column bearing a bronze statue of Justice (1581) stands in the centre. The church of Santa Trinità (see **FLORENCE-CHURCHES 2***) is adjacent.*

PIAZZA SAN LORENZO
One of the liveliest market squares in Florence and the location of the Basilica di San Lorenzo (see **FLORENCE-CHURCHES 1***). See* **FLORENCE-WALK**.

PIAZZA SANTA CROCE
A large rectangular square fronting the church of Santa Croce (see **FLORENCE-CHURCHES 1***). It was the former site of preaching, executions, football games and jousts put on by the Medici (see* **A-Z***). This is the only Florentine square with benches for weary sightseers. See* **FLORENCE-WALK**.

PIAZZA SANTA MARIA NOVELLA
A popular meeting-place for Florentines, overlooked by the magnificent façade of Santa Maria Novella (see **FLORENCE-CHURCHES 1***).*

PIAZZA SANTO SPIRITO
A busy market, shady garden and stately church (see **FLORENCE-CHURCHES 2***) all make this one of the city's most charming squares.*

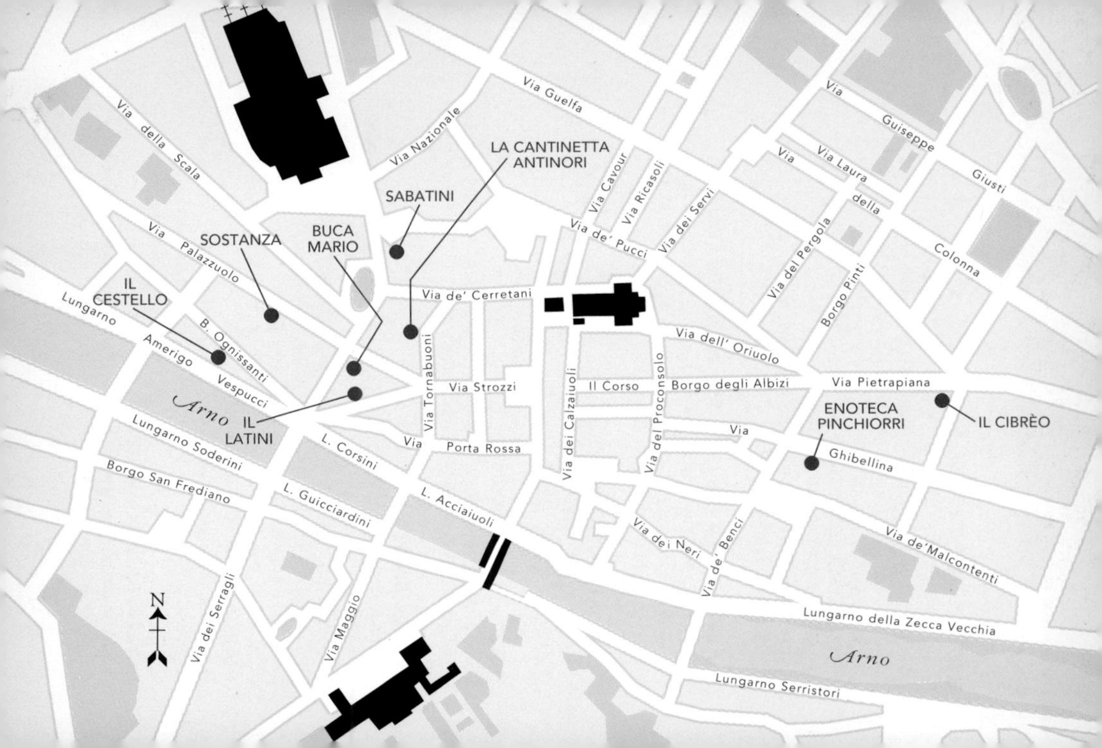
LA CANTINETTA ANTINORI
SABATINI
SOSTANZA
BUCA MARIO
IL CESTELLO
IL LATINI
ENOTECA PINCHIORRI
IL CIBRÈO
Via della Scala
Via Palazzuolo
Via Nazionale
Via Guelfa
Via Cavour
Via Ricasoli
Via dei Servi
Via de' Pucci
Via Giuseppe Giusti
Via Laura
Via della Colonna
Via del Pergola
Borgo Pinti
Via de' Cerretani
Via dell' Oriuolo
Via Pietrapiana
Borgo degli Albizi
Il Corso
Via Strozzi
Via Tornabuoni
Via Porta Rossa
Via dei Calzaiuoli
Via del Proconsolo
Via Ghibellina
Via de'Malcontenti
Via dei Neri
Via de' Benci
Lungarno Amerigo Vespucci
B. Ognissanti
Arno
Lungarno Soderini
Borgo San Frediano
L. Corsini
L. Guicciardini
L. Acciaiuoli
Lungarno della Zecca Vecchia
Lungarno Serristori
Via dei Serragli
Via Maggio
N

ENOTECA PINCHIORRI Via Ghibellina 87, tel: 242777.
■ 1230-1400 Tue.-Sat., 1930-2200 Mon.-Sat. Closed Aug. Booking advised. ● Expensive.
Brilliant Franco-Italian cuisine and wines served in the 15thC Palazzo Ciofi-Lacometti. Try the seven-course Menu di Degustazione.

LA CANTINETTA ANTINORI Piazza Antinori 3.
■ 1200-1430, 1915-2230 Mon.-Fri. ● Expensive.
A congenial wine bar in a fine 17thC palazzo *serving excellent meals.*

SABATINI Via de' Panzani 41.
■ 1200-1430, 1930-2230 Tue.-Sun. ● Expensive.
The city's most elegant restaurant, with the best bistecca alla fiorentina.

IL CESTELLO Hotel Excelsior, Piazza di Ognissanti 3.
■ 1200-1500, 1900-2330. ● Expensive.
Dishes include superb lobster, truffles and local ribollita *(see* **Food***).*

IL CIBRÈO Via de' Macci 118, Piazza Sant'Ambrogio.
■ 1215-1430, 1915-2200 Tue.-Sat. Closed Aug. ● Moderate-Expensive.
Serves nouvelle cuisine, *and good soups and soufflés. The kitchen divides the expensive and budget menu and clientele! No pasta dishes.*

BUCA MARIO Piazza Ottaviani 16-17.
■ 1145-1500 Fri.-Tue., 1930-2400 Thu.-Tue. Closed July. ● Moderate.
A cellar restaurant in the 1886 Palazzo Niccolini offering home-made pasta, good grills and game in season; popular with tourists.

IL LATINI Via Palchetti 6r, off Vigna Nuova.
■ 1230-1430 Wed.-Sun., 1900-2230 Tue.-Sun. ● Moderate.
Four separate rooms cater for up to 200 diners. There are often queues for good noisy meals, including enjoyable Tuscan country cooking.

SOSTANZA Via del Porcellana 25r.
■ 1200-1430 Mon.-Sat., 1930-2130 Mon.-Fri. Closed Aug. ● Moderate.
Typical crowded Tuscan working men's trattoria. Brusque service.

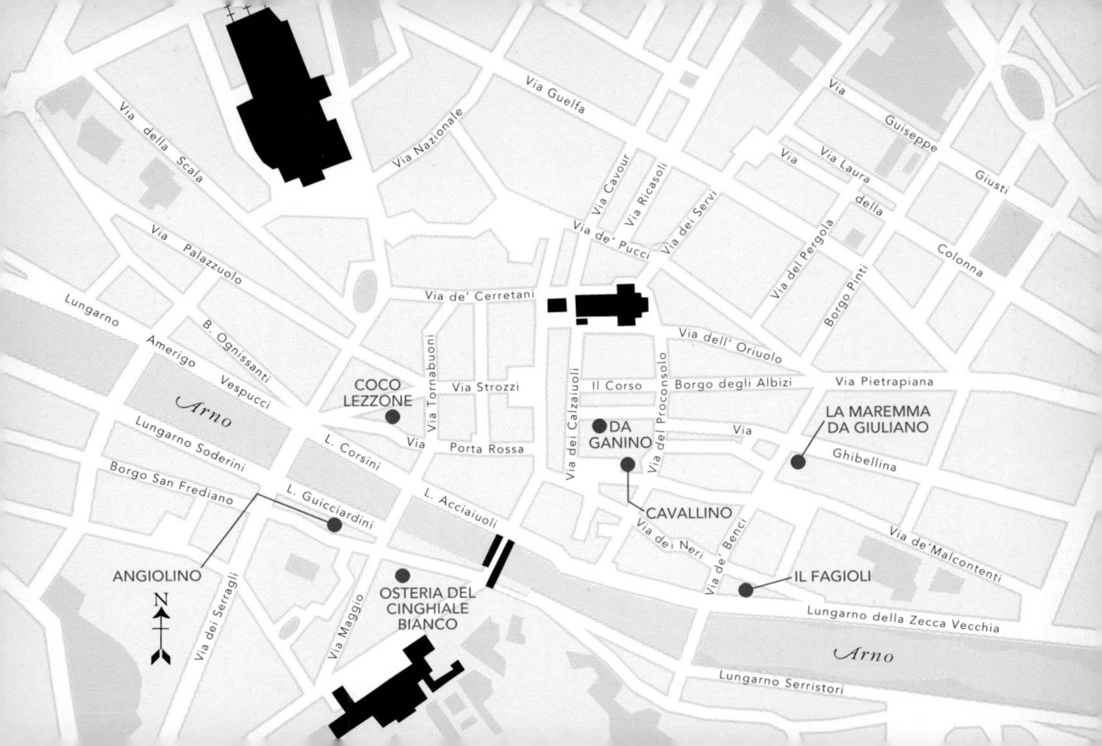

LA MAREMMA DA GIULIANO
IL FAGIOLI
CAVALLINO
DA GANINO
COCO LEZZONE
OSTERIA DEL CINGHIALE BIANCO
ANGIOLINO
N
Arno
Arno
Via della Scala
Via Nazionale
Via Guelfa
Via Palazzuolo
Lungarno Amerigo Vespucci
B. Ognissanti
Lungarno Soderini
Borgo San Frediano
L. Guicciardini
L. Corsini
L. Acciaiuoli
Via dei Serragli
Via Maggio
Via de' Cerretani
Via Tornabuoni
Via Strozzi
Via Porta Rossa
Via dei Calzaiuoli
Il Corso
Via del Proconsolo
Borgo degli Albizi
Via Pietrapiana
Via Ghibellina
Via dell' Oriuolo
Via Cavour
Via Ricasoli
Via dei Servi
Via de' Pucci
Via del Pergola
Borgo Pinti
Via Laura
Via della Colonna
Via Guiseppe Giusti
Via dei Neri
Via de' Benci
Via de'Malcontenti
Lungarno della Zecca Vecchia
Lungarno Serristori

COCO LEZZONE Via del Parioncino 26r, off Via Parion.
1200-1500, 1900-2300 Mon.-Fri. Closed Aug. Moderate.
A chaotic white-tiled trattoria, often crammed full with locals at communal tables. Choose from delicious farfalline *(butterfly-shaped pancakes) with truffles and garlic, rare roast beef or* trippa alla fiorentina *(see* **Food***).*

CAVALLINO Via delle Farine 2-6.
1200-1500, 1900-2200 Tue.-Sun. Moderate.
Large corner restaurant overlooking the Palazzo Vecchio, with a L.27,000 tourist menu. Try the trippa alla fiorentina.

LA MAREMMA DA GIULIANO Via Guiseppe Verdi 16r.
1200-1430, 1900-2130 Fri.-Tue. Closed Aug. Moderate.
A popular family-run trattoria, with good pasta and game dishes, including prosciutto di cinghiale *(wild boar ham).*

ANGIOLINO Via di Santo Spirito 36, Oltrarno.
1100-1500, 1900-2400 Tue.-Sun. Inexpensive.
*A friendly family trattoria; try the meringue cake (*cavour*).*

OSTERIA DEL CINGHIALE BIANCO Borgo San Jacopo 43r, Oltrarno. 1200-1430, 1930-2300 Tue.-Sun. Inexpensive.
Typical medieval Florentine dishes served in a candle-lit 12thC building; English-owned. Wild boar con polenta *is a speciality.*

IL FAGIOLI Corso Tintori 45-47.
1200-1430, 1900-2100 Fri.-Tue. Closed Aug. Inexpensive.
A small friendly Tuscan trattoria with the usual range of pasta and meat dishes.

DA GANINO Piazza Cimatori 4.
1200-1500, 1930-2130 Mon.-Sat. Closed mid Aug. Inexpensive.
An intimate but popular osteria *with a small outdoor terrace. Try the* carpaccio *(beef fillet), the home-made pastas and the* torta di formaggio *(cheese flan).*

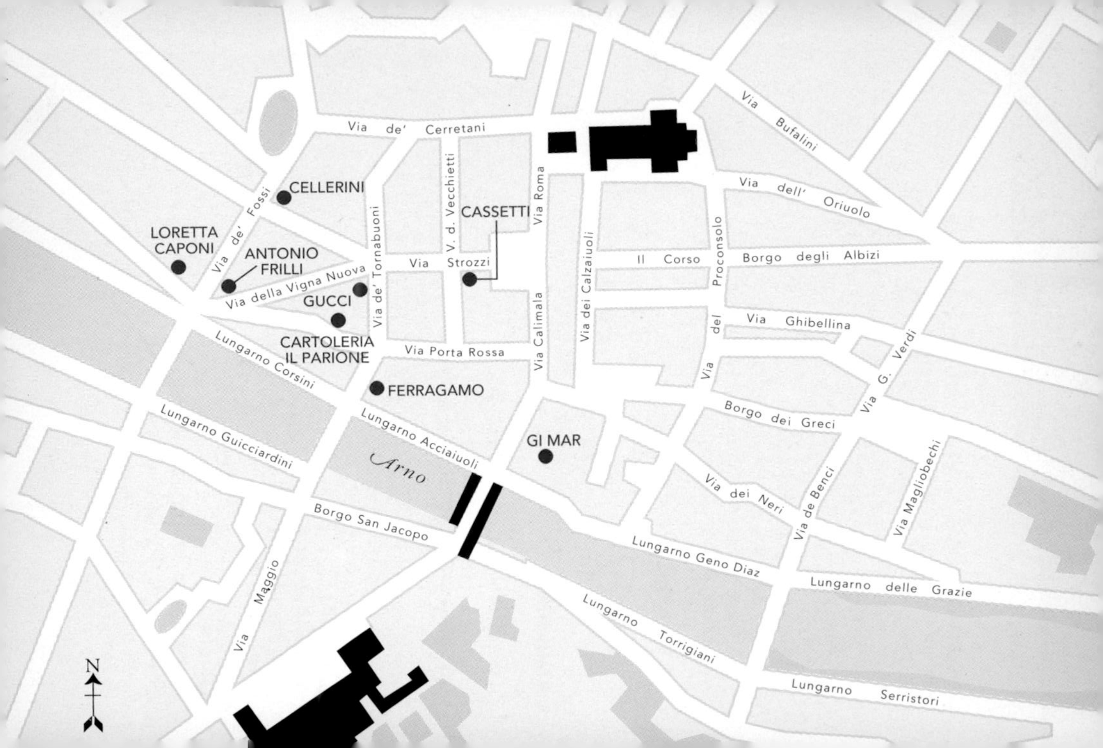
Via de' Cerretani
Via Bufalini
Via dell' Oriuolo
CELLERINI
Via de' Fossi
LORETTA CAPONI
ANTONIO FRILLI
Via della Vigna Nuova
GUCCI
CARTOLERIA IL PARIONE
Via de' Tornabuoni
V. d. Vecchietti
Via Strozzi
CASSETTI
Via Roma
Via dei Calzaiuoli
Il Corso
Proconsolo
Borgo degli Albizi
Via del
Via Ghibellina
Via Calimala
Via Porta Rossa
FERRAGAMO
Lungarno Corsini
Lungarno Guicciardini
Lungarno Acciaiuoli
Arno
GI MAR
Borgo dei Greci
Via G. Verdi
Via dei Neri
Via de Benci
Via Magliobechi
Borgo San Jacopo
Lungarno Geno Diaz
Lungarno delle Grazie
Lungarno Torrigiani
Lungarno Serristori
Via Maggio
N

GUCCI Via Tornabuoni 73-75r.
■ 0930-1300, 1530-1930 Mon.-Sat.
Internationally-renowned boutique famous for its accessories as much as for its clothes. It even sells household goods under its own label!

SALVATORE FERRAGAMO Via Tornabuoni 16.
■ 0930-1930 Tue.-Fri., Sat. am (summer), Mon. pm (winter).
Very chic – and expensive – male and female fashions.

CELLERINI Via del Sole 37r.
■ 0930-1300, 1530-1930 Tue.-Fri., 0930-1300 Sat. (summer), 1530-1930 Mon. (winter).
Leather shop specializing in very smart accessories.

LORETTA CAPONI Borgo Ognissanti 12.
■ 0930-1300, 1600-1900 Tue.-Fri., 0930-1300 Sat. (summer), 1600-1900 Mon. (winter).
Lingerie boutique with exclusive hand-embroidered nightdresses.

CASSETTI Via degli Strozzi 7-9r.
■ 0900-1300, 1600-1900 Mon.-Sat.
Famous throughout Tuscany for the exceptional quality of its silverware.

ANTONIO FRILLI Via de' Fossi 24-26r.
■ 0900 1930 Tue.-Fri., Sat. am (summer), Mon. pm (winter).
An art studio specializing in marbles, bronzes and fine reproductions.

GI MAR Via Lambertesca 22r-26r.
■ 0900-1930 Tue.-Sat.
Art studio selling antique bronzes, marble, crystal, porcelain, ceramics and terracotta objets d'art.

CARTOLERIA IL PARIONE Via del Parione 10r.
■ 0900-1300, 1530-1930 Tue.-Sat.
Exquisite hand-decorated, Florentine-design paper gift items; a truly 'Renaissance' selection!

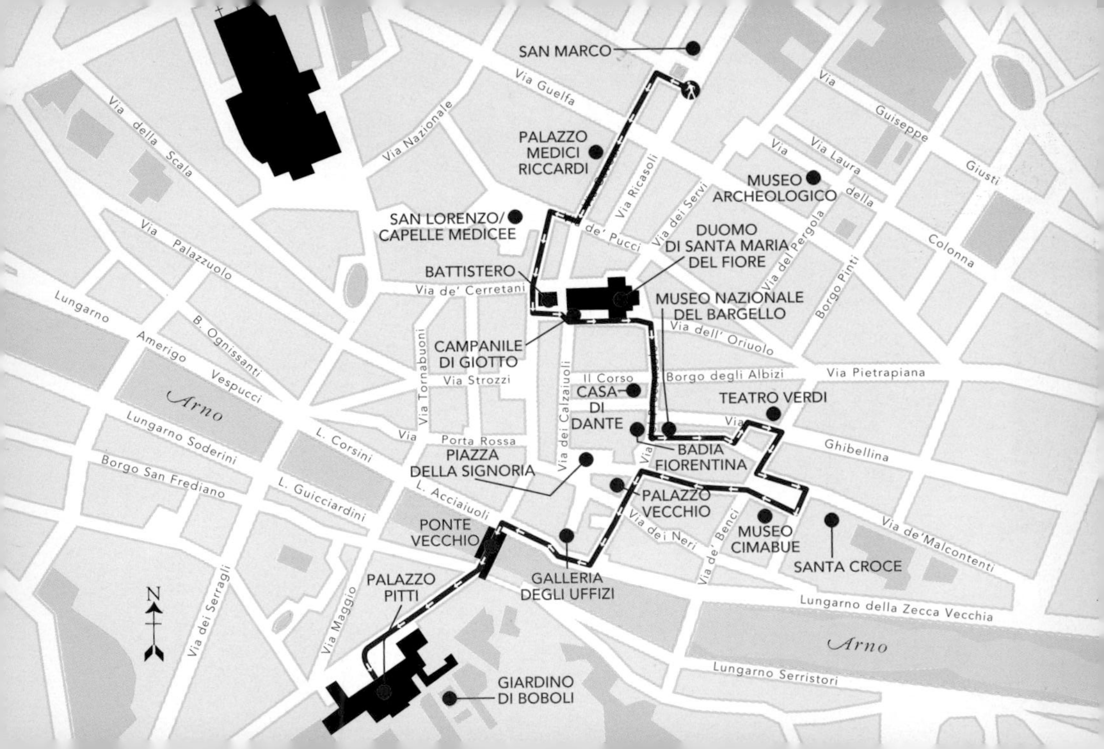
SAN MARCO
PALAZZO MEDICI RICCARDI
SAN LORENZO/ CAPELLE MEDICEE
MUSEO ARCHEOLOGICO
DUOMO DI SANTA MARIA DEL FIORE
BATTISTERO
MUSEO NAZIONALE DEL BARGELLO
CAMPANILE DI GIOTTO
CASA DI DANTE
TEATRO VERDI
BADIA FIORENTINA
PIAZZA DELLA SIGNORIA
PALAZZO VECCHIO
MUSEO CIMABUE
SANTA CROCE
PONTE VECCHIO
GALLERIA DEGLI UFFIZI
PALAZZO PITTI
GIARDINO DI BOBOLI
Via Guelfa
Via della Scala
Via Nazionale
Via Giuseppe Giusti
Via Laura
Via della Colonna
Via Ricasoli
Via dei Servi
de' Pucci
Via del Pergola
Borgo Pinti
Via Palazzuolo
Via de' Cerretani
Lungarno Amerigo Vespucci
B. Ognissanti
Via dell' Oriuolo
Via Pietrapiana
Borgo degli Albizi
Il Corso
Via Strozzi
Via Tornabuoni
Via dei Calzaiuoli
Arno
Lungarno Soderini
L. Corsini
Via Porta Rossa
Via Ghibellina
Borgo San Frediano
L. Guicciardini
L. Acciaiuoli
Via dei Neri
Via de' Benci
Via de'Malcontenti
Lungarno della Zecca Vecchia
Via dei Serragli
Via Maggio
Lungarno Serristori
N

Duration: 3 hr, excluding visits.
The Galleria dell'Accademia di Belle Arti (see **FLORENCE-MUSEUMS 1**) at Via Ricasoli 60 is the starting point. It is near the university and Piazza San Marco, with its convent, cloisters and museum of works by Fra Angelico (see **A-Z**). The Museo Archeologico (see **FLORENCE-MUSEUMS 2**), Via della Colonna 36, with its superb Etruscan sculptures, is 100 m southeast. Cross Piazza San Marco, turn left on Via Cavour and walk southwest for 200 m to the Palazzo Medici Riccardi (see **FLORENCE-PALAZZI**), commissioned by Cosimo de' Medici and built by Michelozzo (1444-60). It now houses the Prefettura but the first-floor treasures can be visited and include Gozzoli's frescoes in the chapel, and Michelangelo's (see **A-Z**) windows. Turn right on Via de' Gori into Piazza San Lorenzo (see **FLORENCE-PIAZZE**) to see the Capelle Medicee by Brunelleschi (see **A-Z**), plus two sacristies and the Laurentian library. Borgo San Lorenzo leads to the west end of Piazza San Giovanni, from where there are astonishing views of the octagonal Battistero (Basilica di San Giovanni) (see **FLORENCE-CHURCHES 1**). Near it in Piazza del Duomo stand the famous bell tower, Campanile di Giotto (see **FLORENCE-CHURCHES 1**), and the Duomo di Santa Maria del Fiore (see **FLORENCE-CHURCHES 1**). Clad in white marble from Carrara, green from Prato and pink from the Maremma, and dominated by Brunelleschi's great dome, this marvellous edifice dominates 'Florence the Divine'. In the corner of the square is the Museo dell'Opera del Duomo (see **FLORENCE-MUSEUMS 2**) which houses most of the original important works from the Duomo, Battistero and Campanile. Leave the piazza at the southeast corner down the narrow Via del Proconsolo, passing the Museo di Antropologia ed Etnologia (0900-1300 Thu.-Sat., Oct.-June; Free) and Palazzo Pazzi on the left. Turn right into Via Dante Alighieri to see Casa di Dante (see **Dante**) on the corner of Via Santa Margherita. Retrace your footsteps and turn right on Via del Proconsolo to see the splendid Badia Fiorentina (see **FLORENCE-CHURCHES 2**) tower on the right and the formidable crenellated façade of the Museo Nazionale del Bargello (see **FLORENCE-MUSEUMS 1**), which has one of the finest sculpture collections in Italy. Now you need to make an important detour. To the left Via della Vigna Vecchia takes you 250 m east to the Teatro Verdi and 100 m south to Piazza Santa Croce (see **FLORENCE-**

PIAZZE) with its fine 13thC Franciscan church in which are the tombs *of* the famous and frescoes *by* the famous. Next door in the refectory and cloisters is the notable Museo Cimabue (see **FLORENCE-MUSEUMS 2**). Take Borgo dei Greci back west into the centre. In Piazza San Firenze is an 18thC baroque church and the Palazzo Gondi, beyond which is the huge, famous Piazza della Signoria (see **FLORENCE-PIAZZE**), dominated by the Palazzo Vecchio. This has been a government 'fortress' for seven centuries and has elegant courtyards, State quarters, great halls and Vasari (see **A-Z**) frescoes. In the square are Palazzo Uguccioni, Raccolta della Ragione, Loggia dei Lanzi and the entry to Piazzale degli Uffizi. The Galleria degli Uffizi (see **FLORENCE-MUSEUMS 1**), designed by Vasari, is one of the most important museums in Europe, for besides a superb collection of the Florentine School, Tuscan painters and 'foreigners' such as Raphael, Titian and Caravaggio, there are works by Rubens, Rembrandt, Cranach, Dürer, Goya and Memling. There are nearly 50 rooms and you will need to make several visits to see everything. Much of Florence's day-to-day business is still conducted in the Piazza della Signoria, undisturbed by Michelangelo's *David* (copy) and the huge Neptune fountain. Keep on towards the river Arno (see **A-Z**) and turn right on the Lungarno Medici to the Ponte Vecchio (1345), occupied originally by tradesmen (tanners, butchers, linen merchants, greengrocers and blacksmiths). Now the little boutiques are mainly silversmiths, goldsmiths and jewellers. A popular pastime is feeding the river fish from midway across, near Benvenuto Cellini's (see **A-Z**) statue. Try to identify Vasari's secret corridor which crosses the Arno to link the Uffizi with your next port of call, the Palazzo Pitti (see **FLORENCE-MUSEUMS 1**). Keep on south along Via Guicciardini to Piazza de' Pitti, to see the grand-ducal Medici (see **A-Z**) residence. You will need a considerable time to examine the eight galleries and museums. Fortunately, the Boboli gardens (Giardino di Boboli) (the main gate is to the left of Palazzo Pitti) are huge, peaceful and lovely, and contain, besides the amphitheatre, cypress alley and Neptune's fountain, a Kaffeehaus of 1776 with perhaps the best views of all Florence and the Arno. Oltrarno, the working-class neighbourhood west of Palazzo Pitti, has a number of delightful, good-value *trattorie*, including Cammillo, Carmino, Celestino, Mamma Gina and Le Quattro Stagioni.

iardino di Boboli

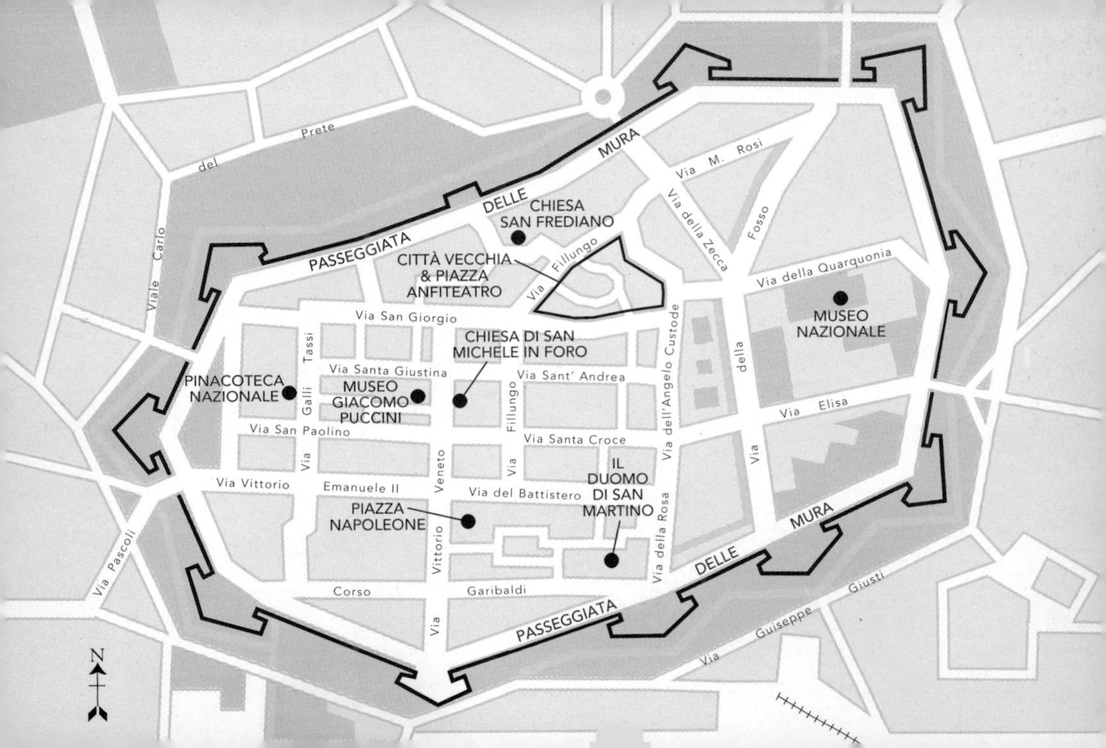

Viale Carlo del Prete
PASSEGGIATA DELLE MURA
CHIESA SAN FREDIANO
Via M. Rosi
Via della Zecca
Via del Fosso
CITTÀ VECCHIA & PIAZZA ANFITEATRO
Via Fillungo
Via della Quarquonia
MUSEO NAZIONALE
Via San Giorgio
CHIESA DI SAN MICHELE IN FORO
Via Santa Giustina
Via Sant' Andrea
Via dell'Angelo Custode
PINACOTECA NAZIONALE
MUSEO GIACOMO PUCCINI
Via Galli Tassi
Via Fillungo
Via Elisa
Via San Paolino
Via Santa Croce
Via Veneto
IL DUOMO DI SAN MARTINO
Via Vittorio Emanuele II
Via del Battistero
PIAZZA NAPOLEONE
Via Vittorio Veneto
Via della Rosa
Via Pascoli
Corso Garibaldi
PASSEGGIATA DELLE MURA
Via Guiseppe Giusti
N

IL DUOMO DI SAN MARTINO Piazza San Martino.
■ 0700-1200, 1530-1830 Mar.-Sep., 0700-1200, 1500-1730 Oct.-Feb.
Mainly 11th-13thC, it has the tomb of del Carreto, a Ghirlandaio Madonna, *Tintoretto's* The Last Supper *and the famous* Volto Santo.

CHIESA DI SAN MICHELE IN FORO Piazza San Michele.
■ 0700-1200, 1530-1830 Mar.-Sep., 0700-1200, 1500-1730 Oct.-Feb.
Romanesque church with a sculpture of archangel Michael on top of the façade. See works by Lippi and Civitali, and a Madonna *by della Robbia.*

CHIESA DI SAN FREDIANO Piazza San Frediano.
■ 0700-1200, 1530-1830 Mar.-Sep., 0700-1200, 1500-1730 Oct.-Feb.
Basilica of 1112-47, restored in honour of the Irish St. Frigidian. Note the façade mosaics and the mummified Santa Zita (Virgin saint of Lucca).

PINACOTECA NAZIONALE Palazzo Mansi, Via Galli Tassi 43.
■ 0900-1400 Tue.-Sat., 0900-1300 Sun. ● L.6000.
Renaissance paintings and drawings. See Tintoretto's Miracle of St. Mark.

MUSEO NAZIONALE Villa Guinigi, Via della Quarquonia.
■ 0900-1400 Tue.-Sat., 0900-1300 Sun. ● L.5000.
Etruscan and Roman pieces, as well as works by Lucchese sculptors.

MUSEO GIACOMO PUCCINI Via di Poggio.
■ 1000-1800 April-Sep., 1000-1600 Nov. Mar. ● Free.
The composer's house, containing his Steinway piano and mementos.

PIAZZA NAPOLEONE
Large tree-lined square with a statue of Bonaparte's sister. Contains the Palazzo Ducale (1579), now the Prefettura, and the Teatro del Giglio.

CITTÀ VECCHIA & PIAZZA ANFITEATRO
Medieval palazzi *and streets surrounding the Roman amphitheatre site.*

PASSEGGIATA DELLE MURA
4.2 km walk with superb views, where half the town gossips and flirts!

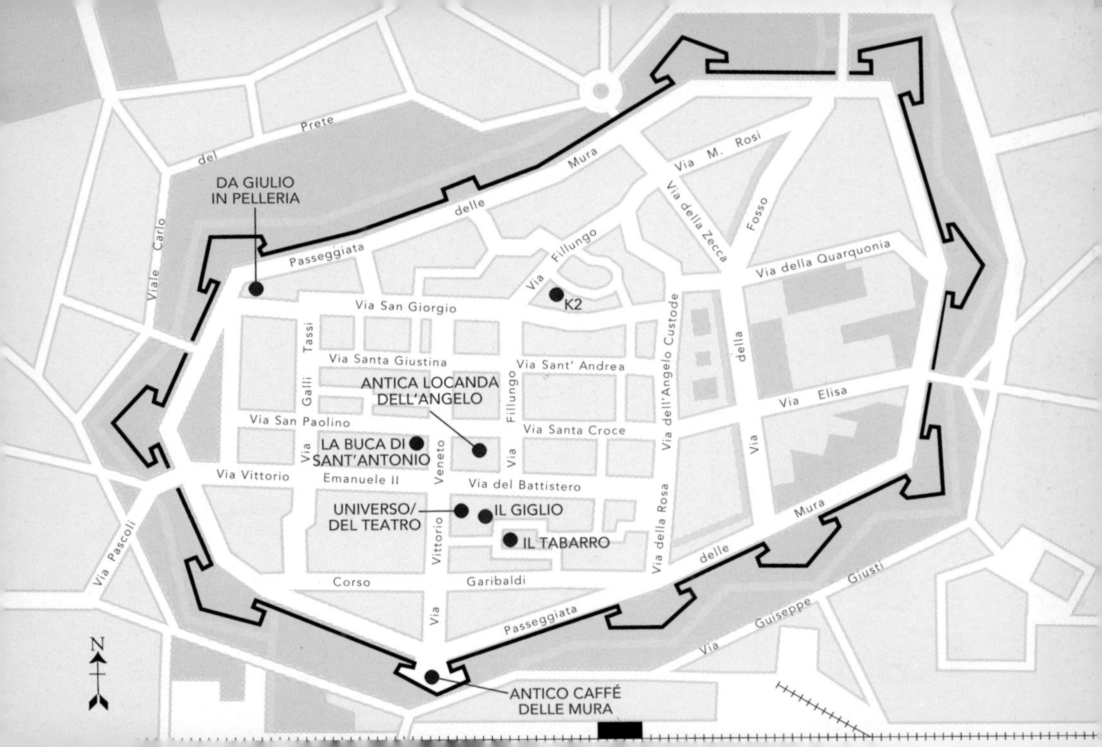
DA GIULIO
IN PELLERIA
K2
ANTICA LOCANDA
DELL'ANGELO
LA BUCA DI
SANT'ANTONIO
UNIVERSO/
DEL TEATRO
IL GIGLIO
IL TABARRO
ANTICO CAFFÉ
DELLE MURA
Viale Carlo del Prete
Passeggiata delle Mura
Via M. Rosi
Via della Zecca
Fosso
Via della Quarquonia
Via Fillungo
Via San Giorgio
Via Tassi
Via Galli
Via Santa Giustina
Via Sant' Andrea
Via San Paolino
Via Santa Croce
Via dell'Angelo Custode
Via della Rosa
Via della Fosso
Via Elisa
Via Veneto
Via Vittorio Emanuele II
Via del Battistero
Via Vittorio
Corso Garibaldi
Via Pascoli
Via Guiseppe Giusti
N

LA BUCA DI SANT'ANTONIO Via della Cervia 1-5.
1245-1400 Tue.-Sun., 1945-2100 Tue.-Sat. Closed mid July.
Expensive.
The best in Lucca! Gourmet restaurant founded in 1787 offering a L.30,000 tourist menu.

IL TABARRO 9-10 Piazza del Giglio.
1300-1400 Tue.-Sun., 2015-2230 Tue.-Sat. Expensive.
In business since 1414, the restaurant is in a mansion with a courtyard. Smart and popular, it offers filletto grigoa *and* carbonara di mare.

ANTICA LOCANDA DELL'ANGELO Via Pescheria 21.
1300-1400 Tue.-Sun., 2000-2115 Tue.-Sat. Moderate.
Genuine Lucchese cuisine. Try the coniglio alla cacciatora con olive.

UNIVERSO/DEL TEATRO Piazza del Giglio.
1100-1600, 1800-0100 Fri.-Wed. Moderate.
Trattoria in a large orange-coloured mansion offering a L.25,000 tourist menu. Try the totani alla griglia *(cuttlefish).*

DA GIULIO IN PELLERIA Piazza San Donato 49.
1300-1415, 2015-2130 Tue.-Sat. Closed Aug. Moderate.
Good-value Tuscan dishes and a wide range of wines in a handsome building near the northwestern ramparts.

ANTICO CAFFÉ DELLE MURA Piazzale Vittorio Emanuele 4.
1245-1400, 2000-2130 Tue.-Sun. Moderate.
Pretty porticoed façade and marble tables. Try the rabbit dishes.

IL GIGLIO Piazza del Giglio.
1245-1415 Thu.-Tue., 1945-2130 Thu.-Mon. Moderate.
Despite its peeling façade, a popular restaurant for freshwater fish dishes.

K2 Via dell'Anfiteatro 107.
1100-1500, 1800-0100 Thu.-Tue. Inexpensive.
A good-value, basic ristorante *with pasta and pizza dishes.*

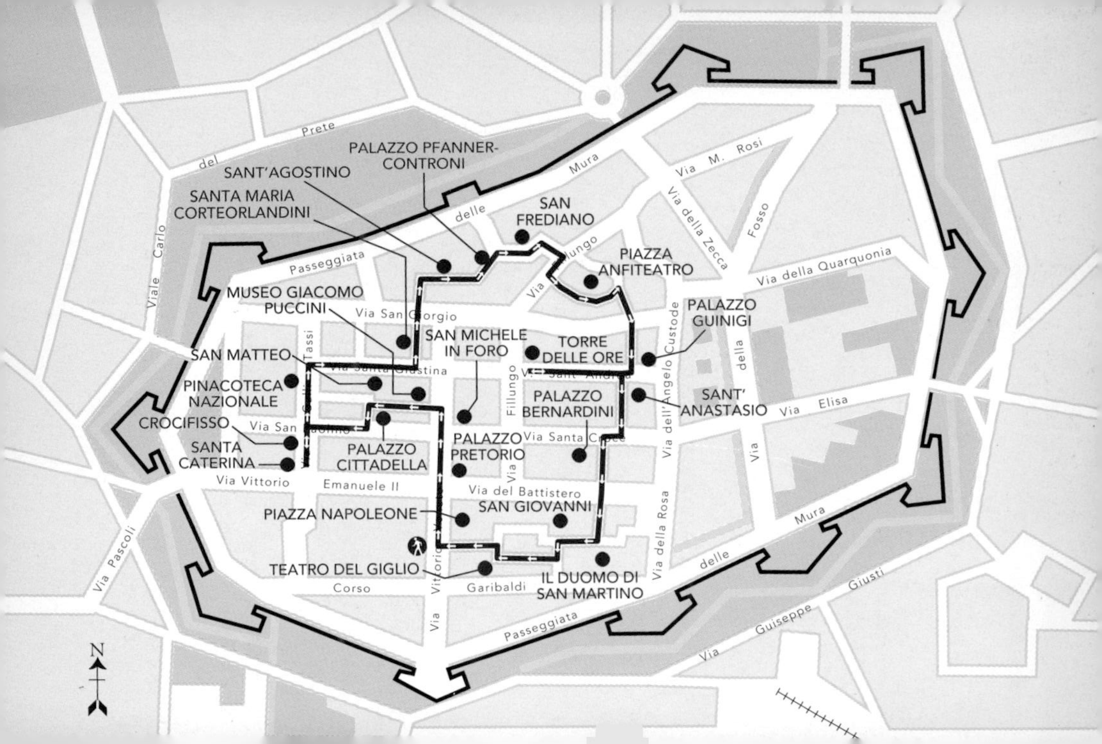
PALAZZO PFANNER-CONTRONI
SANT'AGOSTINO
SANTA MARIA CORTEORLANDINI
SAN FREDIANO
PIAZZA ANFITEATRO
MUSEO GIACOMO PUCCINI
PALAZZO GUINIGI
SAN MICHELE IN FORO
TORRE DELLE ORE
SAN MATTEO
PINACOTECA NAZIONALE
PALAZZO BERNARDINI
SANT' ANASTASIO
CROCIFISSO
SANTA CATERINA
PALAZZO CITTADELLA
PALAZZO PRETORIO
SAN GIOVANNI
PIAZZA NAPOLEONE
TEATRO DEL GIGLIO
IL DUOMO DI SAN MARTINO
N
Via del Prete
Viale Carlo
Mura delle
Passeggiata
Via M. Rosi
Via della Zecca
Fosso
Via della Quarquonia
Via Fillungo
Via San Giorgio
Via Santa Giustina
Via Santa Croce
Via dell'Angelo Custode
Via della
Via Elisa
Via del Battistero
Via della Rosa
Via Vittorio Emanuele II
Via Pascoli
Corso Garibaldi
Mura delle
Passeggiata
Via Guiseppe Giusti
Via San Paolino
Via Tassi
Via Sant' Andrea

Duration: 3 hr.
Begin at the tourist office at Via Vittorio Veneto 46, just north of the Palace of Justice in Piazzale Vittorio Emanuele. Turn left into the Piazza Napoleone (see **LUCCA-ATTRACTIONS**) with the Prefettura and courtyard on your left, and the statue of Elisa Baciocchi, patron and Princess of Lucca, and Napoleon's sister, in the centre of the square. Keep north past Palazzo Pretorio (1492) with its fine loggia, into Piazza San Michele. This attractive square is where the citizens of Lucca assemble during the evening. The Chiesa di San Michele in Foro (see **LUCCA-ATTRACTIONS**) has a statue of St. Michael between two angels killing a dragon. The square, which was originally the Roman forum, is surrounded by a series of beautiful *palazzi*, now owned by Tuscan banks. Every 12 July the Palio della Balestra, a crossbow competition, takes place here. Turn left on Via di Poggio and visit the Museo Giacomo Puccini (see **LUCCA-ATTRACTIONS**) and Palazzo Cittadella. Next go half-left into Via San Paolino to Via Galli Tassi. On the left are the Crocifisso and Santa Caterina churches. However, turn right to see the 17thC Palazzo Mansi, now the Pinacoteca Nazionale (see **LUCCA-ATTRACTIONS**), and admire the bridal room with its delicate, canopied, baroque four-poster. Keep on Via Galli Tassi then turn right on Via Santa Giustina. The church of San Matteo is on the right. Keep on for 200 m to Palazzo Orsetti on the corner of Via di Loreto, and see the church of Santa Maria Corteorlandini. Cross Via San Giorgio to Piazza Sant'Agostino, the ramparts and the church of Sant'Agostino with its attractive campanile and cupola. Keep roughly parallel to the ramparts on Via C. Battisti past

Palazzo Pfanner-Contror

the large Palazzo Pfanner-Controni (0900-1400 Tue.-Sun.; L.5000), a costume museum set in lovely gardens, to Piazza del Collegio and Piazza San Frediano. The 12thC Chiesa di San Frediano (see **LUCCA-ATTRACTIONS**) with its three large Pisan doors, high campanile, Berlinghieri's mosaics, Romanesque font and the relic of Santa Zita, deserves a visit. Head southeast for 200 m, across Via Fillungo, where you should see the superb 13thC Casa Barbetti-Barboni at No. 43 and the Torre delle Ore opposite, to the Roman amphitheatre, now Piazza Anfiteatro (see **LUCCA-ATTRACTIONS**), which is a bit seedy but has several good restaurants. It is then a further 250 m across Via A. Mordini to the 14thC Palazzo Guinigi (1000-1630; L.5500). Look out for the mature oak trees growing on top of its two towers. The *palazzo* is a complex of red-brick and white marble-columned medieval palaces, of which Nos 20 and 29 belonged to the despotic Guinigi family in the early 15thC. Continue south on the narrow Via Sant'Anastasio past two oratories (Sant'Anastasio and Santa Guilia) and the Suffragio to the Palazzo Bernardini on the right. Go through Piazza dei Servi, where there are two churches (San Benedetto in Gottella and Santa Maria dei Servi), to Piazza Antelminelli, where you can see the sides of Il Duomo di San Martino (see **LUCCA-ATTRACTIONS**) and the church of San Giovanni. After admiring these two fine buildings, particularly the savage animal frieze on the Duomo façade and the holy relic, *Volto Santo*, an 11thC effigy of Christ which is carried through the streets on 13 Sep. in a major procession to and from San Frediano, walk 200 m to the west to little Piazza del Giglio, in which are the Teatro del Giglio (where Puccini concerts are held in summer) and a number of good restaurants (see **LUCCA-RESTAURANTS**). Return to Piazza Napoleone and back to the tourist office where the walk began.

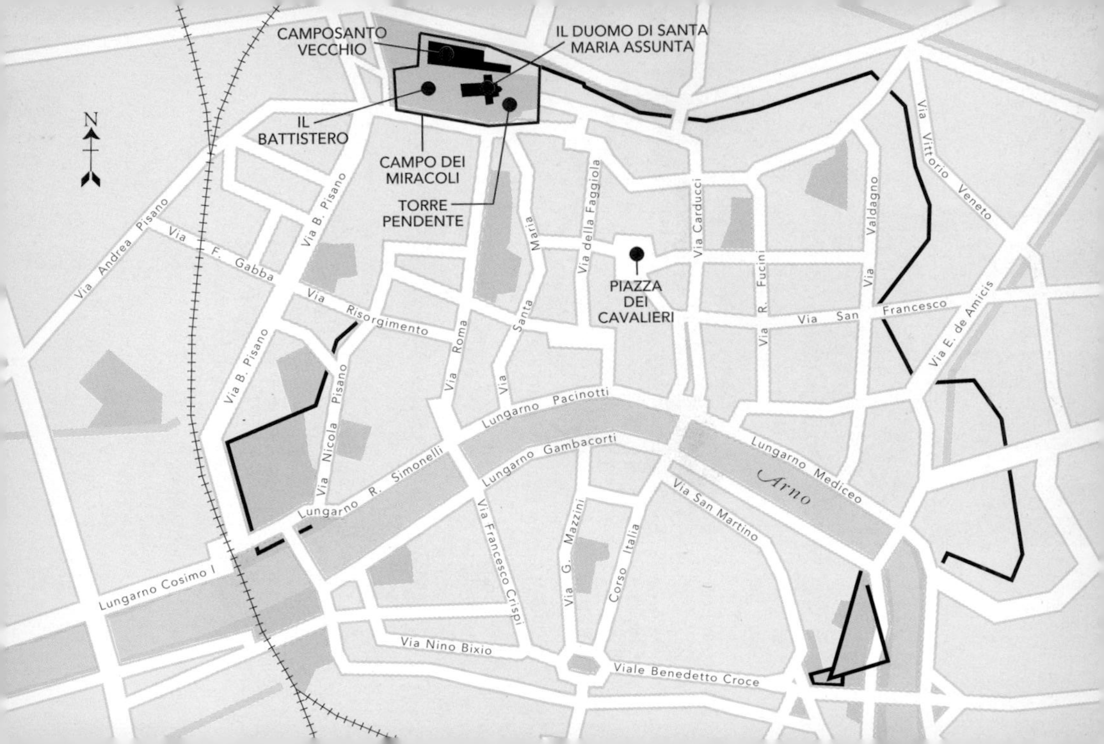
CAMPOSANTO VECCHIO
IL DUOMO DI SANTA MARIA ASSUNTA
IL BATTISTERO
CAMPO DEI MIRACOLI
TORRE PENDENTE
PIAZZA DEI CAVALIERI
N
Via Andrea Pisano
Via F. Gabba
Via B. Pisano
Via Risorgimento
Via Nicola Pisano
Via Roma
Via Santa Maria
Via della Faggiola
Via Carducci
Via R. Fucini
Via Valdagno
Via San Francesco
Via Vittorio Veneto
Via E. de Amicis
Lungarno Pacinotti
Lungarno Gambacorti
Lungarno R. Simonelli
Lungarno Cosimo I
Lungarno Mediceo
Arno
Via San Martino
Via Francesco Crispi
Via G. Mazzini
Corso Italia
Via Nino Bixio
Viale Benedetto Croce

CAMPO DEI MIRACOLI Piazza del Duomo.
Four of the world's architectural and cultural marvels (see below); a complex of ivory-marble buildings on brilliant green turf, within 13thC walls.

IL DUOMO DI SANTA MARIA ASSUNTA Piazza del Duomo.
■ 0800-1940 April-Sep., 0900-1740 Mar. & Oct., 0900-1645 Nov.-Feb.
● Duomo Free, Treasury L.4000.
Started in 1064, its black and white façade was completed in the 12thC. Note Pisano's pulpit, his masterpiece, in the centre, and his fine bronze doors at the south end, paintings by Andrea del Sarto and Cimabue, and Galileo's bronze lamp. The sacristy contains the cathedral's treasury.

IL BATTISTERO Piazza del Duomo.
■ 0800-1940 April-Sep., 0900-1740 Mar. & Oct., 0900-1645 Nov.-Feb.
● L.6000.
Begun in 1152, it was completed in the 14thC. Another fine Pisano pulpit (1260), da Como's octagonal font (1246) and many panels, sculptures and statues should be seen. The building possesses excellent acoustics.

TORRE PENDENTE (CAMPANILE) Piazza del Duomo.
■ Closed, perhaps permanently, for 'repairs'.
This circular, white-marble, 56 m-high bell tower (1179-1350) now leans nearly 5 m from the perpendicular. A spiral staircase of 294 steps leads to the top, from where Galileo (see **A-Z***) is said to have dropped metal balls in order to disprove Aristotle's theories.*

CAMPOSANTO VECCHIO Piazza del Duomo.
■ 0900-1700. ● L.6000.
A white-walled cemetery with 13thC 'holy earth' brought by the Crusaders. Although damaged in World War II, there still remain many frescoes by Gaddi, Aretino and Gozzoli, plus sarcophagi and sculptures.

PIAZZA DEI CAVALIERI
Vasari built this elegant square for the Knights of St. Stephen. Note the Palazzo dei Cavalieri (1562), with busts of six Medici grand dukes, San Stefano dei Cavalieri church (1569) and Palazzo dell'Orologio (1607).

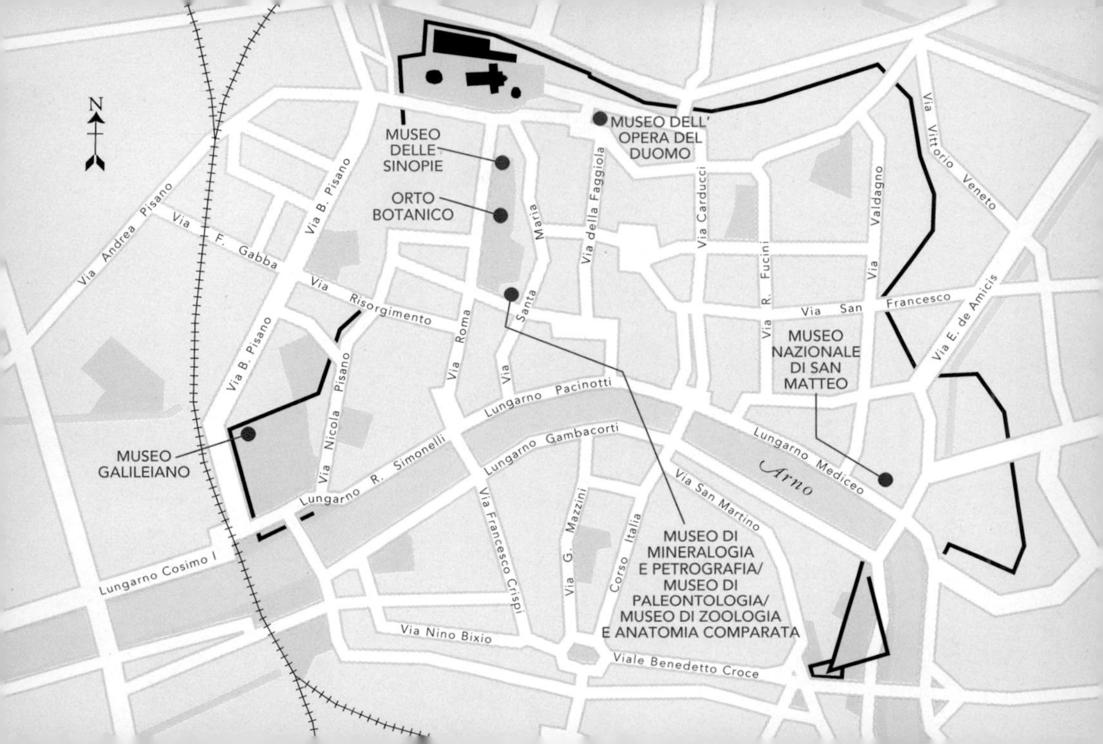
N
MUSEO DELLE SINOPIE
ORTO BOTANICO
MUSEO DELL' OPERA DEL DUOMO
MUSEO NAZIONALE DI SAN MATTEO
MUSEO GALILEIANO
MUSEO DI MINERALOGIA E PETROGRAFIA/ MUSEO DI PALEONTOLOGIA/ MUSEO DI ZOOLOGIA E ANATOMIA COMPARATA
Arno
Via Andrea Pisano
Via F. Gabba
Via B. Pisano
Via Risorgimento
Via Nicola Pisano
Via Roma
Via Santa Maria
Via della Faggiola
Via Carducci
Via R. Fucini
Via Valdagno
Via San Francesco
Via Vittorio Veneto
Via E. de Amicis
Lungarno Pacinotti
Lungarno Gambacorti
Lungarno R. Simonelli
Lungarno Mediceo
Lungarno Cosimo I
Via Francesco Crispi
Via G. Mazzini
Corso Italia
Via San Martino
Via Nino Bixio
Viale Benedetto Croce

MUSEO NAZIONALE DI SAN MATTEO Piazza San Matteo.
■ 0900-1300, 1500-1800 Tue.-Sat., 0900-1300 Sun. ● L.6000.
Painted panels, sculptures and an altarpiece by Masaccio, plus works by the Pisano family and Simone Martini, in a Benedictine monastery with 15thC cloisters.

MUSEO DELL'OPERA DEL DUOMO Palazzo dell Primaziale, Piazza Arcivescovado.
■ 0900-1900. ● L.6000.
11th-13thC sculptures, treasure, ancient robes, illuminated manuscripts and 16th-18thC paintings displayed in the Bishop's Palace. The museum also has Etruscan and Roman archaeological sections.

MUSEO DELLE SINOPIE Piazza del Duomo.
■ 0900-1245, 1500-1845. ● L.6000.
Sketches (sinopie) *of important 14th-15thC frescoes in the Ospedale Nuovo della Misericordia.*

MUSEO GALILEIANO Piazza Macelli, off Via N. Pisano.
■ 0900-1200, 1500-1800 Mon.-Sat. ● L.5000.
The Galileo (see **A-Z**) *museum houses a library with old editions of the mathematician's work. He was born in Pisa in 1564.*

MUSEO DI MINERALOGIA E PETROGRAFIA
MUSEO DI PALEONTOLOGIA
MUSEO DI ZOOLOGIA E ANATOMIA COMPARATA
Via Santa Maria 53.
■ 0900-1200, 1500-2000 Mon.-Fri. Ring bell and ask to view.
Three specialist museums run by the university. The first has a collection of Tuscan minerals, the second deals with the prehistory of the region and the third is a natural history museum linked with the Santa Croce monastery.

ORTO BOTANICO Via Ghini 5.
■ 0800-1300 Mon.-Sat., 1400-1730 Mon.-Fri. ● L.6000.
These botanical gardens are the setting for a natural history museum.

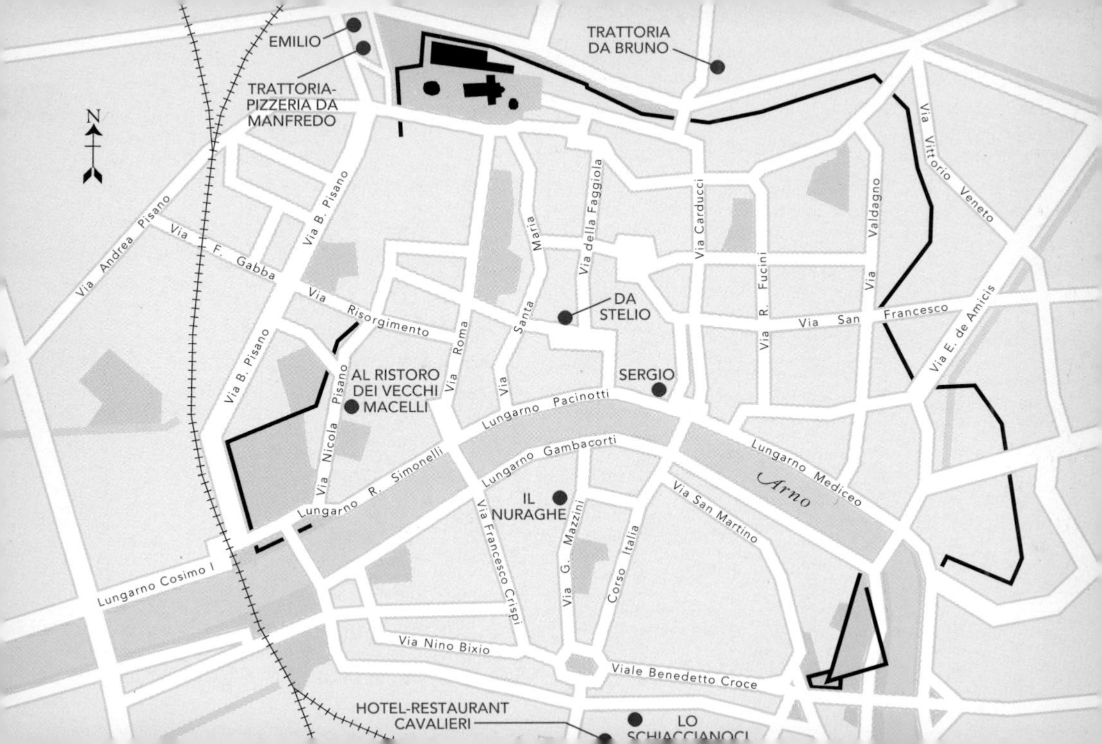
EMILIO
TRATTORIA-PIZZERIA DA MANFREDO
TRATTORIA DA BRUNO
N
DA STELIO
SERGIO
AL RISTORO DEI VECCHI MACELLI
IL NURAGHE
HOTEL-RESTAURANT CAVALIERI
LO SCHIACCIANOCI
Arno
Via Andrea Pisano
Via F. Gabba
Via B. Pisano
Via Risorgimento
Via Nicola Pisano
Via Roma
Via Santa Maria
Via della Faggiola
Via Carducci
Via R. Fucini
Via Valdagno
Via San Francesco
Via Vittorio Veneto
Via E. de Amicis
Lungarno Pacinotti
Lungarno Gambacorti
Lungarno R. Simonelli
Lungarno Mediceo
Lungarno Cosimo I
Via Francesco Crispi
Via G. Mazzini
Corso Italia
Via San Martino
Via Nino Bixio
Viale Benedetto Croce

Restaurants

SERGIO Lungarno Pacinotti 1-2.
■ 1230-1415 Tue.-Sat., 2000-2145 Mon.-Sat. ● Expensive.
Top class with views over the yellow Arno. L.90,000 fixed-price menu.

AL RISTORO DEI VECCHI MACELLI Via Volturno 49.
■ 1245-1415 Mon., Tue. & Thu.-Sat., 2000-2200 Thu.-Tue. Closed Aug. ● Expensive.
Modest restaurant in a quiet side street; superb cooking. Worth finding.

HOTEL-RESTAURANT CAVALIERI Piazza Stazione 2.
■ 1200-1430, 1945-2145. ● Moderate.
International cuisine and good service. Has a L.40,000 menu, inc. wine.

EMILIO Via Carlo Cammeo 46.
■ 1245-1500, 2030-2215 Tue.-Sun. ● Moderate.
Large, smart restaurant. The tourist menu, at L.30,000, is good value.

IL NURAGHE Via Guiseppe Mazzini 58.
■ 1300-1430, 2015-2200 Tue.-Sun. ● Moderate.
Restaurant in a quiet side street offering excellent L.25,000 tourist menu.

TRATTORIA DA BRUNO Via Luigi Bianchi 12.
■ 1245-1500 Wed.-Sun., 2000-2215 Wed.-Mon. ● Moderate.
Large, popular and smart; try the squid. The tourist menu costs L.30,000.

LO SCHIACCIANOCI Via Amerigo Vespucci 104.
■ 1230-1415, 1930-2200 Mon.-Sat. ● Moderate.
Unassuming establishment which serves good Tuscan cuisine and wines.

TRATTORIA-PIZZERIA DA MANFREDO Via Carlo Cammeo 43. ■ 1245-1500, 2000-2145 Tue.-Sun. ● Moderate.
The tourist menu includes scaloppine alla pizzaiola *and* cervello fritto.

DA STELIO Piazza Dante 11.
■ 1200-1600 Mon.-Sat., 1800-2400 Mon.-Fri. ● Inexpensive.
Hearty student or impoverished tourist fare, including pastas and pizzas.

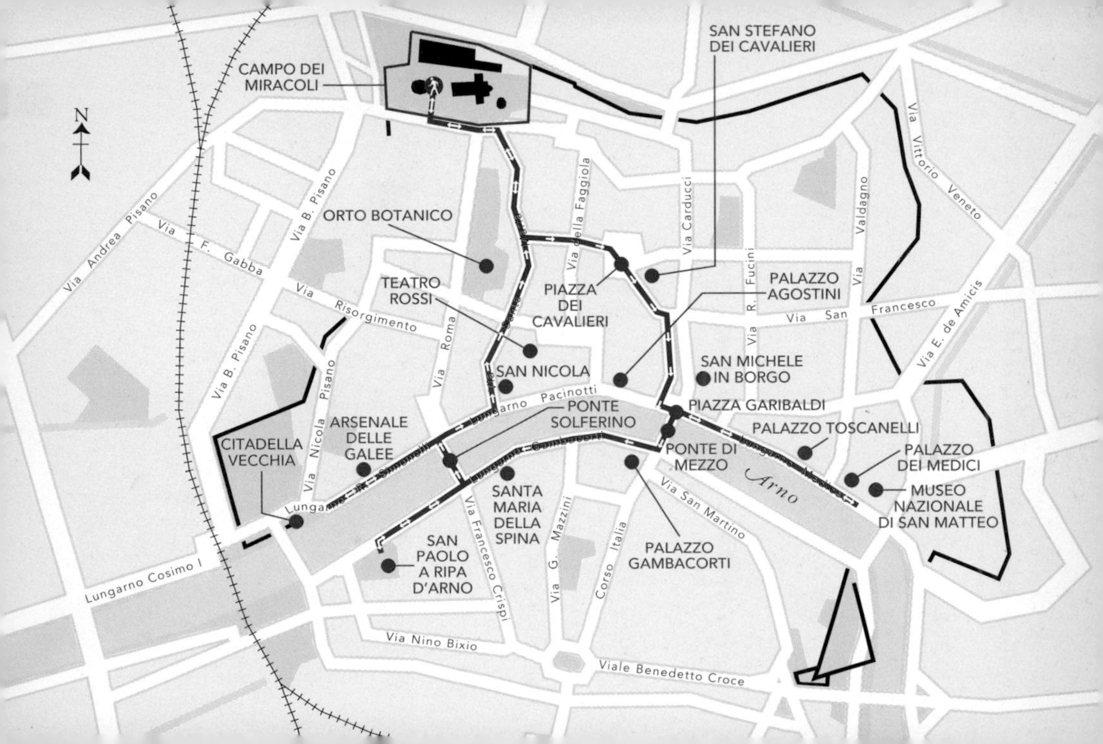
N
CAMPO DEI MIRACOLI
SAN STEFANO DEI CAVALIERI
ORTO BOTANICO
TEATRO ROSSI
PIAZZA DEI CAVALIERI
PALAZZO AGOSTINI
SAN NICOLA
SAN MICHELE IN BORGO
PIAZZA GARIBALDI
PONTE SOLFERINO
PALAZZO TOSCANELLI
ARSENALE DELLE GALEE
CITADELLA VECCHIA
PONTE DI MEZZO
PALAZZO DEI MEDICI
MUSEO NAZIONALE DI SAN MATTEO
SANTA MARIA DELLA SPINA
SAN PAOLO A RIPA D'ARNO
PALAZZO GAMBACORTI
Arno
Via Andrea Pisano
Via F. Gabba
Via B. Pisano
Via Risorgimento
Via Nicola Pisano
Via Roma
Via della Faggiola
Via Carducci
Via R. Fucini
Via Valdagno
Via San Francesco
Via Vittorio Veneto
Via E. de Amicis
Lungarno Pacinotti
Lungarno Cosimo I
Via Francesco Crispi
Via G. Mazzini
Corso Italia
Via San Martino
Via Nino Bixio
Viale Benedetto Croce

Walk

Duration: 3 hr, excluding visits.
Start at the Campo dei Miracoli, having explored the spectacular Duomo and Battistero, visited the Museo delle Sinopie and Museo dell'Opera del Duomo and studied the awesome tilt of the Torre Pendente (see **PISA-ATTRACTIONS**, **MUSEUMS**). Don't be put off by the hordes of (fellow) tourists and the dozens of curio shops and stalls. The above may have taken all morning, so this gentle walk through the rest of Pisa is not too demanding.
From the southeast corner head south on Via Santa Maria into Piazza Cavallotti, and just before the Orto Botanico (see **PISA-MUSEUMS**) turn left on Via dei Mille past the church of San Sisto into Piazza dei Cavalieri (see **PISA-ATTRACTIONS**). Admire the Palazzo della Carovana, Vasari's (see **A-Z**) Palazzo dei Cavalieri (who fought the Saracens), the church of San Stefano dei Cavalieri (with Crusader trophies) and, on the north side, the sinister but delightful Palazzo dell'Orologio with its two towers, where the mad Count Ugolino is reputed to have starved his children and then eaten them! Head for the river Arno (see **A-Z**) on Via Dini, and the narrow Via Notari to Piazza Garibaldi. Visit the church of San Michele in Borgo, built in the 9thC over a temple dedicated to Mars, which is in the arcaded main street of Borgo Stretto, 100 m to the north. To your left along the north bank of the river are the Palazzo Toscanelli where Lord Byron once lived, and which now houses the State archives; the Teatro Verdi; tourist office; 13thC Palazzo dei Medici (Prefettura); and the Museo Nazionale di San Matteo (see **PISA-MUSEUMS**); all within a 400 m walk. Immediately to the right are the excellent restaurant Sergio (see **PISA-RESTAURANTS**); the old-fashioned Grand Hotel Victoria; Palazzo Agostini; the Teatro Rossi; the university buildings; and the main town markets tucked away in Piazza Vettovaglie (0900-1230 Mon.-Sat.). After pursuing these various detours, continue across the oldest bridge, Ponte di Mezzo, the focal point for the Gioco del Ponte and the Regatta di San Ranieri, when the four town quarters each sponsor a boat. The railway station and the large Piazza Vittorio Emanuele II are respectively 800 m and 600 m due south. However, turn right and walk along the banks of the river past the Palazzo and Loggia Gambacorti (town hall) for 300 m to the rather startling, ornate, white-marble Chiesa Santa Maria della Spina

Il Battistero

(open am only, no services). This beautiful oratory (1325) is adorned with Pisano (see **A-Z**) sculptures and statues. The story goes that a Pisan merchant brought back from the Holy Land a thorn from Christ's crown – hence the name (*spina*). Because of flooding, the church was raised by a metre, stone by stone, in 1871. Further west down the river are the Romanesque church of San Paolo a Ripa d'Arno, dating from the 9thC, with a superb façade, and behind it, 12thC Sant'Agata. Recross the river at the Ponte Solferino. Downriver are the Arsenale delle Galee and the Citadella Vecchia (1405). Turn right and walk along the Lungarno Pacinotti for 200 m, then turn left on Via Santa Maria past the 12thC church of San Nicola, with works by Pisano and an octagonal leaning campanile. To the north are the three university museums (see **PISA-MUSEUMS**) and the delightful Orto Botanico again. Three hundred metres further on is the Campo dei Miracoli, from where the walk started.

Torre Pendente

N
Via Cavallotti
MUSEO DELL'
OPERA DEL DUOMO
Via R. Luti
Via Curtatone
Via San Fabiano
Via del Seminario
Via San
Antonio
Gobetti
Via San Vincenzo
Via L. Muzzi
IL DUOMO DI
SANTO STEFANO
MUSEO DI
PITTURA MURALE
Via C. Guasti
PALAZZO
COMUNALE
Via Cavour
Via Banchelli
PALAZZO
PRETORIO
Via Cairoli
Via Matteotti
Bisenzio
Via Bruno Buozzi
Via G. Verdi
Via Ricasoli
Via Santa Caterina
Via Dante
BASILICA DI SANTA
MARIA DELLE CARCERI
CHIESA DI SAN
FRANCESCO
Via San Jacopo
Via Piave
Via Cavour
CASTELLO
DELL'
IMPERATORE
Via Santa Chiara
Viale Vittorio Veneto
Via SS Trinita
Via Frascati
Via G. Carradori
Via Pomeria
Via Pomeria

IL DUOMO DI SANTO STEFANO Piazza del Duomo. ■ 0630-1200, 1530-1830. *Built in the 14thC with black and white marble walls, it contains works by Filippo Lippi (*John the Baptist *and* Salome*); a Donatello pulpit; della Robbia terracottas; chapel of the Sacred Girdle.*

BASILICA DI SANTA MARIA DELLE CARCERI
Piazza Santa Maria delle Carceri. ■ 0630-1200, 1630-1900.
A masterpiece of Renaissance architecture, designed by Giuliano da Sangallo. Note the della Robbia blue and white terracotta decorations.

CHIESA DI SAN FRANCESCO Piazza San Francesco.
■ 0630-1130, 1600-1900. *The green and white marble façade was built in 1294. Note the 14thC frescoes in the convent chapterhouse,* St. Matthew as a Moneychanger *and Datini's tomb.*

MUSEO DELL'OPERA DEL DUOMO Piazza del Duomo 49.
■ 0930-1230 Wed.-Mon., 1500-1830 Mon. & Wed.-Sat. ● Combined ticket L.6000. *See Maso di Bartolomeo's reliquary of the Holy Girdle (1446) and the Michelozzo pulpit in the old Bishop's Palace.*

MUSEO DI PITTURA MURALE Piazza San Domenico 8.
■ 0900-1200 Wed.-Mon. ● Combined ticket L.6000.
Unusual collection of wall paintings by Gaddi, Gerini, Uccello, etc.

PALAZZO PRETORIO Galleria Comunale, Piazza del Comune.
■ 0900-1300, 1500-1900. ● Combined ticket L.6000.
Lippi's works feature in this municipal art collection in a 13thC palazzo.

PALAZZO COMUNALE Piazza del Comune.
■ 0900-1300. Admission by request. ● Free.
The huge council hall has frescoes and portraits of Tuscan grand dukes.

CASTELLO DELL'IMPERATORE Via Serlapo Mazzei 41.
■ 0830-1230, 1500-1700 Wed.-Mon. ● Free when no 'shows' are on.
Built in 1248 for Emperor Frederick II in the Norman style, and unique in Tuscany. Used for art exhibitions, concerts and plays. Rampart walks.

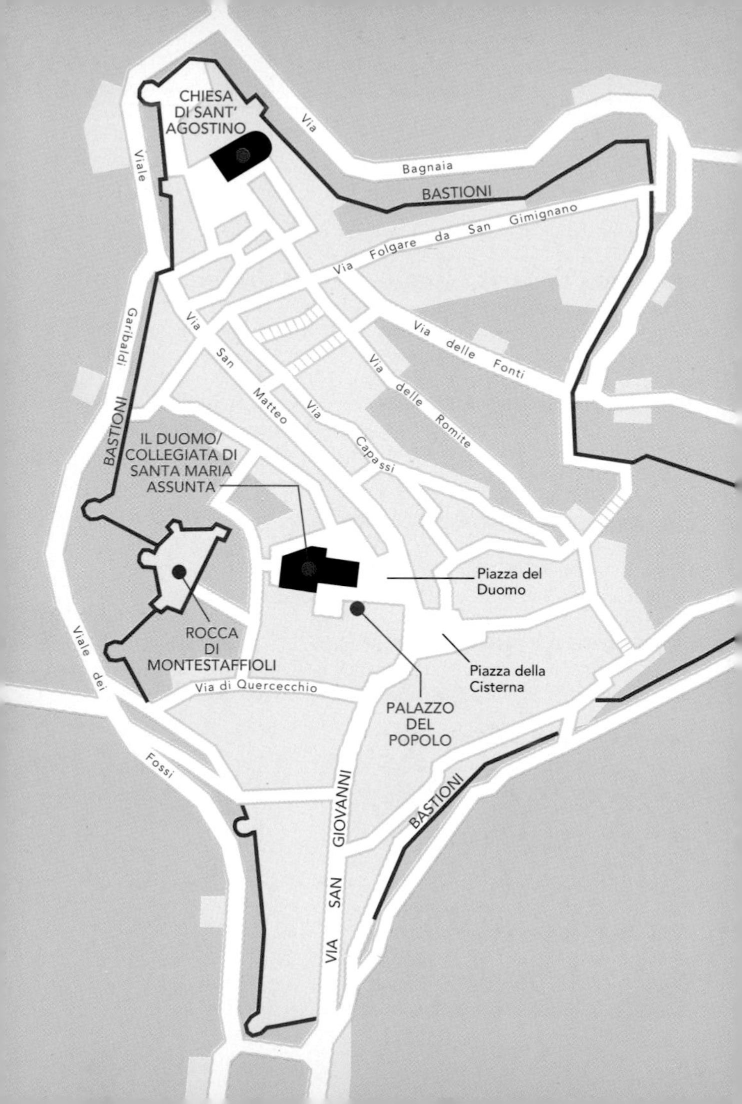
CHIESA
DI SANT'
AGOSTINO
Via
Bagnaia
BASTIONI
Viale
Via Folgare da San Gimignano
Via delle Fonti
Via delle Romite
Via San Matteo
Via Capassi
Viale Garibaldi
BASTIONI
IL DUOMO/
COLLEGIATA DI
SANTA MARIA
ASSUNTA
Piazza del
Duomo
ROCCA
DI
MONTESTAFFIOLI
Piazza della
Cisterna
Via di Quercecchio
PALAZZO
DEL
POPOLO
Viale dei Fossi
BASTIONI
VIA SAN GIOVANNI

RAMPARTS (BASTIONI)
Ramparts, bastions and 15 of the original 76 medieval towers have survived, saved by the town's poverty (it wasn't worth attacking) in the Middle Ages. A total of over 2 km of ramparts afford superb views across the nearby vineyards.

IL DUOMO/COLLEGIATA DI SANTA MARIA ASSUNTA
Piazza del Duomo.
Built in 1148, though much restored, the Romanesque interior has frescoes by Bara da Siena and Bartolo di Fredi. Note the Capella di Santa Fina with frescoes by Ghirlandaio (see **A-Z***).*

PALAZZO DEL POPOLO Piazza del Cisterna.
■ Museo Civico 0930-1230, 1500-1800 Tue.-Sun.
This magnificent 13thC palazzo *houses the town offices, Museo Civico and a courtyard with coats of arms, frescoes, and a well dating from 1360. It is overlooked by the 54 m-high Torre del Podesta, built in 1311, which can be climbed by the more active.*

CHIESA DI SANT'AGOSTINO Piazza Agostino.
Built in 1298 in Romanesque/Gothic style, the church has 17 fine frescoes by Gozzoli. The Capella di San Bartolo has an altar of 1494 by Da Maiano and there are also 15thC cloisters.

ROCCA DI MONTESTAFFIOLI 200 m west of Il Duomo.
Climb the steep hill from Piazza del Duomo to the remains of this fortress built in 1353, from where there are splendid views over the countryside and ideal picnic spots.

VIA SAN GIOVANNI
This is the town's main street which runs north to south from Porta San Giovanni, the finest of the town gates (built in 1262), to Piazza della Cisterna. Along its 400 m length are many artisan shops, the Hotel-Restaurant Bel Soggiorno at No. 41, and several cantinas where the excellent DOC Vino de Gimignano is available.

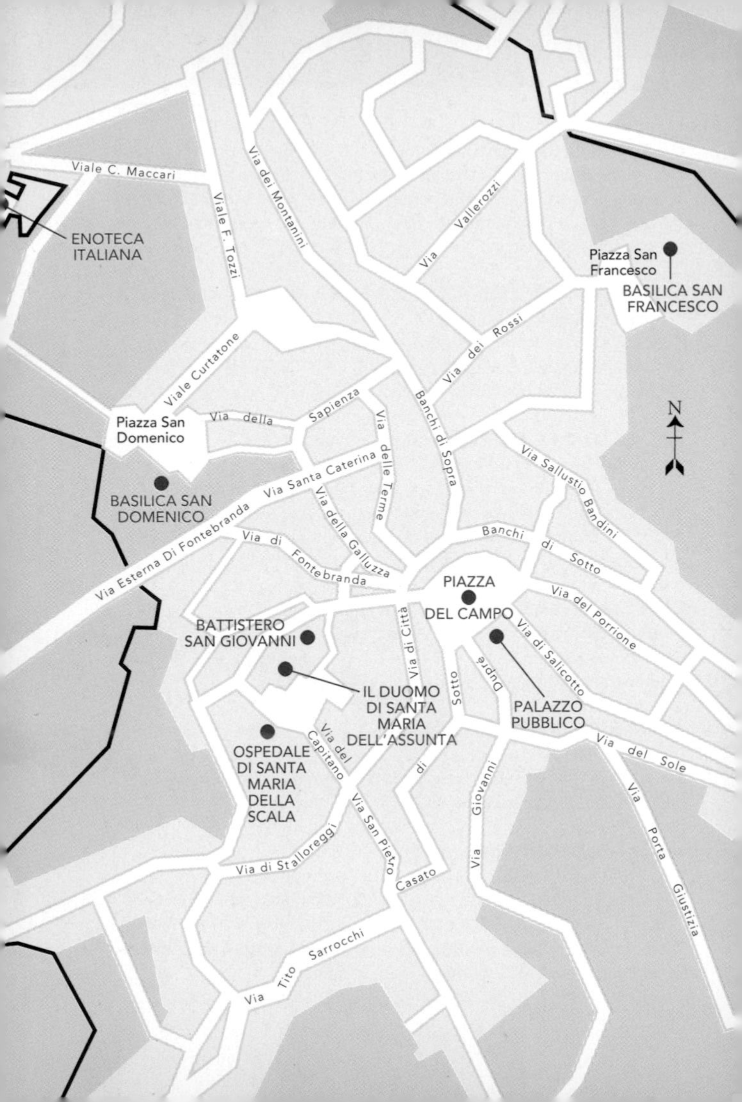
Viale C. Maccari
ENOTECA
ITALIANA
Viale F. Tozzi
Via dei Montanini
Via Vallerozzi
Piazza San
Francesco
BASILICA SAN
FRANCESCO
Via dei Rossi
Viale Curtatone
Piazza San
Domenico
Via della Sapienza
Via delle Terme
Banchi di Sopra
N
Via Sallustio Bandini
Via Santa Caterina
BASILICA SAN
DOMENICO
Via della Galluzza
Banchi di Sotto
Via Esterna Di Fontebranda
Via di Fontebranda
PIAZZA
DEL CAMPO
Via del Porrione
BATTISTERO
SAN GIOVANNI
Via di Città
Via di Salicotto
Dupre
Sotto
IL DUOMO
DI SANTA
MARIA
DELL'ASSUNTA
PALAZZO
PUBBLICO
Via del Capitano
Via del Sole
OSPEDALE
DI SANTA
MARIA
DELLA
SCALA
di
Via Giovanni
Via Porta Giustizia
Via San Pietro
Via di Stalloreggi
Casato
Via Tito Sarrocchi

PIAZZA DEL CAMPO *At the apex of this large shell-shaped sloping square stands the incomparable Palazzo Pubblico, surrounded by medieval buildings, including Palazzo Sansedoni (see* SIENA-PALAZZI*).*

PALAZZO PUBBLICO Piazza del Campo. ■ 0830-1945. Closed Sun. pm. ● L.7000. *Elegant town hall (1297-1342) containing Museo Civico (see* SIENA-MUSEUMS*), picture gallery and Cappella di Piazza. 503 steps up the Torre del Mangia give stunning views (1000-1815; L.4000).*

IL DUOMO DI SANTA MARIA DELL'ASSUNTA Piazza del Duomo. ■ Duomo 0730-1830, Crypt 1000-1300, 1430-1800. ● Duomo Free, Crypt L.3500. *Richly decorated 12th-14thC building faced in black and white striped marble, with an hexagonal cupola and elegant campanile. Note Pisano's (see* **A-Z***) fine pulpit and the engraved marble floor designs. See* SIENA-MUSEUMS.

BATTISTERO SAN GIOVANNI Piazza San Giovanni. ■ 0900-1300, 1500-1700. *Has a Gothic façade, 15thC frescoes, hexagonal font, Donatello statues, a central marble tabernacle and six bronze panels.*

BASILICA SAN DOMENICO Piazza San Domenico. ■ 0730-1830. *Gloomy church built 1266-1465. See Sodoma's frescoes, Renaissance tabernacle, and 14thC crypt and chapel of St. Catherine.*

BASILICA SAN FRANCESCO Viale San Francesco. ■ 0730-1830. *14th-17thC church with notable frescoes by the Lorenzetti family.*

OSPEDALE DI SANTA MARIA DELLA SCALA Piazza del Duomo. ■ 0900-1200 Wed. & Fri., tel: 299410 to view. ● Free, though the porter expects a gratuity. *A medieval hospital which is still in use. Try to see the Sala d'Infermeria and the frescoes by Lorenzo di Pietro and della Quercia. See* SIENA-MUSEUMS.

ENOTECA ITALIANA Fortezza Medicea. ■ 1500-2400. ● Free. *A permanent wine exhibition housed in a medieval fortress where all the best Italian wines can be tasted and purchased.*

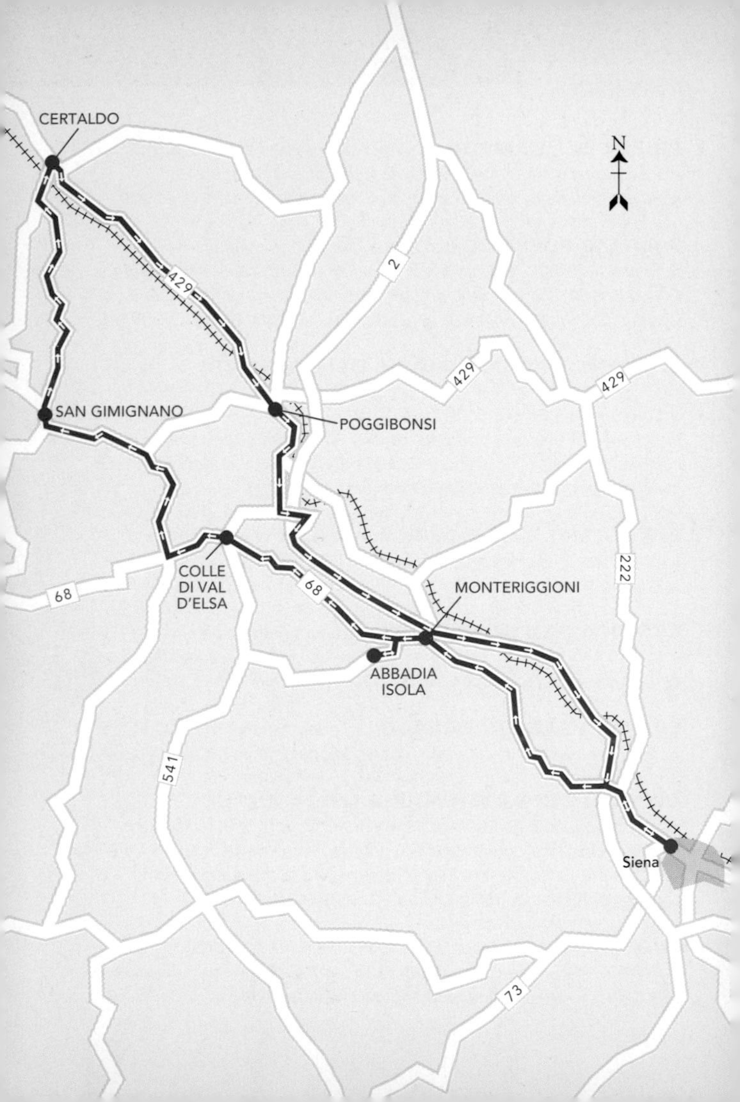

CERTALDO
N
429
2
SAN GIMIGNANO
POGGIBONSI
429
429
COLLE
DI VAL
D'ELSA
68
68
222
MONTERIGGIONI
ABBADIA
ISOLA
541
Siena
73

Excursion

A one-day excursion to San Gimignano and Certaldo.

Leave Siena past the station on Viale Sardegna signposted Firenze (Florence). After 2 km fork left on the SS 2 signposted Poggibonsi. Pass under the autostrada and continue for 13 km.
15 km – Monteriggioni. Pop: 6600. A narrow road to the right leads up to this medieval hill village, completely encircled by 13thC walls built by the Sienese as a defence against Florentine troops. Dante (see **A-Z**), in his *Inferno,* compared the 14 towers to giants. The small Il Poggio restaurant is recommended. Rejoin the SS 2 then fork left on the SS 68, signposted Volterra. After 2 km turn left and make a small detour.
18 km – Abbadia Isola. This Cistercian abbey has an altarpiece (1471) by Sano di Pietro, a Taddeo di Bartolo fresco and a 15thC font. Rejoin the SS 68 and continue northwest.
30 km – Colle di Val d'Elsa. Pop: 15,700. The medieval upper town, Colle Alta, is well worth a visit. (Colle Bassa is the industrial lower town, well known for its fine crystal glassware.) Behind the 13thC fortifications are the Palazzo Campana (1539); Palazzo Pretorio (15thC), which houses the Antiquario Etrusco (1000-1200, 1600-1900 Tue.-Sat.; L.5000); the baroque Duomo (1619); and Palazzo Vescovile, Via del Castello 27, in which there is the little Museo Civico (0900-1200, 1400-1700 Tue.-Sun.; L.5000). Via della Volte and Via del Castello have many attractive houses with coats of arms on the walls. The Ristorante La Vecchia Cartiera, Via Oberdan 5-9, is in an old paper mill and serves good Tuscan dishes. Three kilometres west on the SS 68 take a road north for 10 km, signposted San Gimignano.
43 km – San Gimignano (see SAN GIMIGNANO-ATTRACTIONS, **A-Z**). This is the most attractive hill town in Tuscany – perhaps in Italy. You will need 2-3 hr to explore all the architectural delights. Parking is possible outside the town walls near the main Porta San Giovanni, built in 1262. Continue north for 13 km. This is a pleasant drive through an unspoilt Tuscan countryside of low hills with vines and olives, and occasional red-roofed farms.
56 km – Certaldo. Pop: 16,000. Despite being damaged in World War II, the medieval red-brick village on the hill, Certaldo Alto, where Boccaccio (see **A-Z**) lived and died, is most attractive. It overlooks the

San Gimignan

new town, built in the valley of the river Elsa, which markets excellent Tuscan wines. In the old town see the 15thC Palazzo Pretorio (0900-1230, 1330-1800 Tue.-Sun.; L.3500) in Piazzetta del Vicariato, with its pretty courtyard, loggia, chapel and Etruscan museum complete with frescoes. Also visit Boccaccio's much-restored 13thC house (0900-1200, 1500-1900; L.3500) at Via Boccaccio 18, and the 13thC church and cloister of SS Michele e Jacopo in Via Rivellino, with della Robbia (see **A-Z**) terracottas, 14thC frescoes and Boccaccio's renovated cenotaph. The Osteria del Vicario, near Palazzo Pretorio, serves simple inexpensive fare. Return to Siena on the SS 429, adding just one brief stop.

69 km – Poggibonsi. Pop: 26,000. Badly damaged in World War II, this industrial town produces furniture and chianti wines. Only Palazzo Pretorio and the rebuilt church of San Lorenzo have survived. It is then 30 km back to Siena (99 km).

San Gimignano

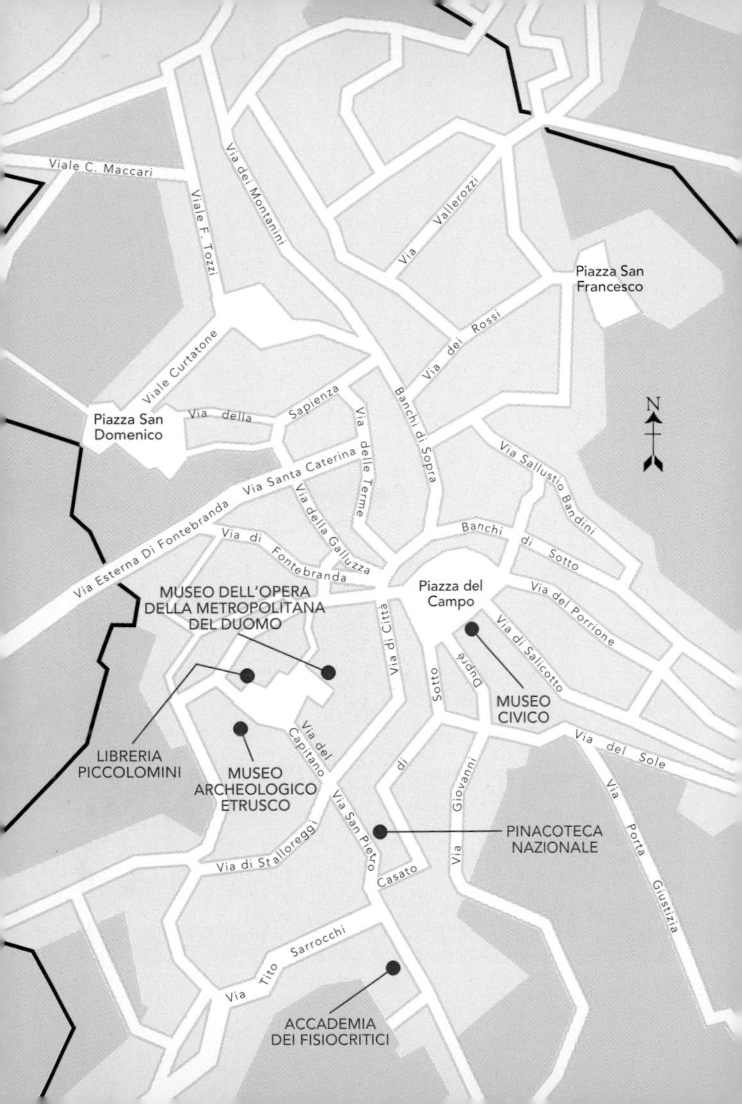

Viale C. Maccari
Viale F. Tozzi
Via dei Montanini
Via Vallerozzi
Piazza San Francesco
Via dei Rossi
Viale Curtatone
Piazza San Domenico
Via della Sapienza
Via delle Terme
Banchi di Sopra
N
Via Santa Caterina
Via Esterna Di Fontebranda
Via della Galluzza
Via Sallustio Bandini
Banchi di Sotto
Via di Fontebranda
Piazza del Campo
MUSEO DELL'OPERA DELLA METROPOLITANA DEL DUOMO
Via del Porrione
Via di Città
Via di Salicotto
Dupre
Sotto
MUSEO CIVICO
Via del Capitano
LIBRERIA PICCOLOMINI
MUSEO ARCHEOLOGICO ETRUSCO
Via del Sole
di
Via Giovanni
Via San Pietro
Via Porta Giustizia
PINACOTECA NAZIONALE
Via di Stalloreggi
Casato
Via Tito Sarrocchi
ACCADEMIA DEI FISIOCRITICI

MUSEO CIVICO Palazzo Pubblico (1st floor), Piazza del Campo 1.
■ 0930-1945. ● L.7000.
See the frescoes in the Sala del Risorgimento; choir stalls, gates and frescoes in the antechapel; Simone Martini equestrian portrait in the Sala del Mappamondo; a Lorenzetti portrait in the Sala della Pace; and works by 14thC Sienese painters in the Sala dei Pilastri. See SIENA-ATTRACTIONS.

LIBRERIA PICCOLOMINI Inside the Duomo, Piazza del Duomo.
■ 0900-1930. ● L.3000.
The famous Piccolomini library founded by Pope Pius III in 1495 has 10 Pinturicchio frescoes, Bregno's Piccolomini altar (1503) and statues by Michelangelo (see **A-Z**). See SIENA-ATTRACTIONS.

MUSEO DELL'OPERA DELLA METROPOLITANA DEL DUOMO Duomo Nuovo, Piazza del Duomo.
■ 0900-1930 summer, 0900-1400 winter. ● L.6000.
See Duccio's Maestà, *works by S. Martini and Lorenzetti, and Pisano figures in the replacement cathedral abandoned after the 1348 plague.*

PINACOTECA NAZIONALE Palazzo Buonsignori, Via San Pietro.
■ 0830-1400 Mon., 0830-1900 Tue.-Sun. am. ● L.9000.
This 14thC palazzo *houses a vast array of 12th-17thC Sienese paintings by Duccio di Buoninsegna, Simone Martini, Guido da Siena, Lorenzetti (see* **A-Z**), *Sodoma, Beccafumi and Pinturicchio. This is a treasure house of talent which will need more than one visit.*

MUSEO ARCHEOLOGICO ETRUSCO Ospedale di Santa Maria della Scala, Piazza del Duomo.
The museum is being reorganized. Check opening times and admission charges with the tourist office, tel: 49153. See SIENA-ATTRACTIONS.

ACCADEMIA DEI FISIOCRITICI Piazza Sant'Agostino 4.
■ 0900-1300 Mon.-Fri., 1500-1800 Mon.-Wed. & Fri. ● Free.
The palazzo *contains three museums – zoological, mineralogical and palaeontological – founded in 1691, plus a science library with 6000 mainly 17th-19thC volumes.*

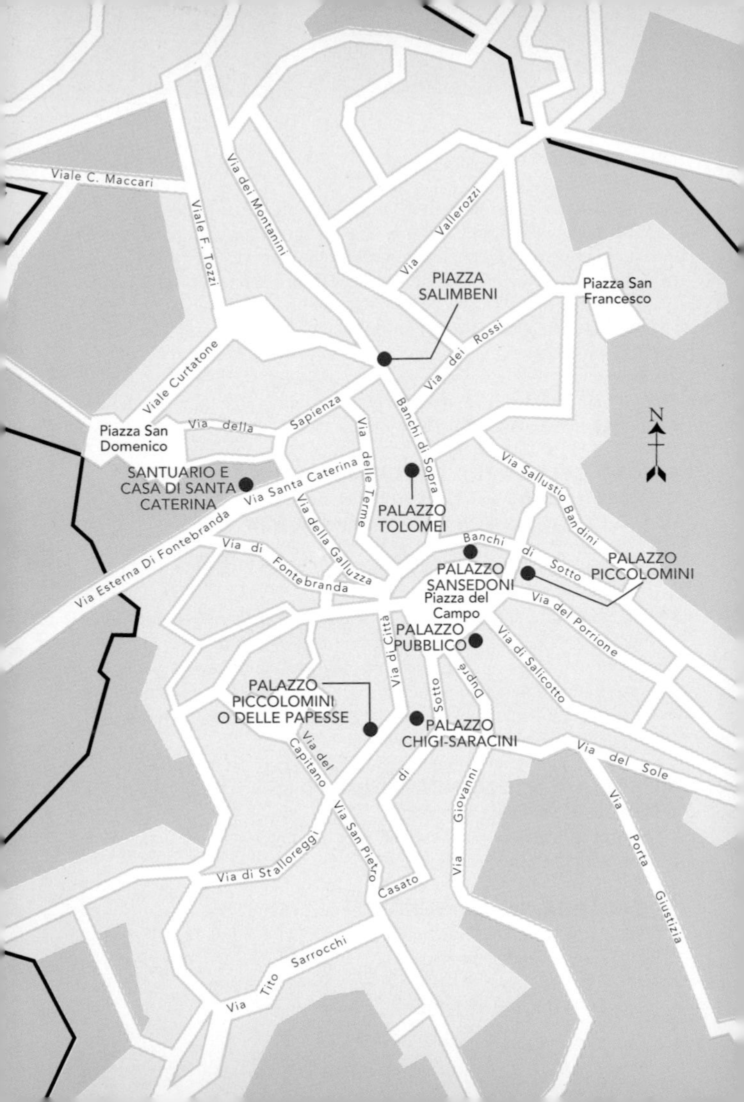
Viale C. Maccari
Viale F. Tozzi
Via dei Montanini
Via Vallerozzi
PIAZZA SALIMBENI
Piazza San Francesco
Via dei Rossi
Viale Curtatone
Piazza San Domenico
Via della Sapienza
Banchi di Sopra
Via delle Terme
SANTUARIO E CASA DI SANTA CATERINA
Via Santa Caterina
PALAZZO TOLOMEI
Via Sallustio Bandini
N
Via della Galluzza
Via di Fontebranda
Via Esterna Di Fontebranda
Banchi di Sotto
PALAZZO SANSEDONI
PALAZZO PICCOLOMINI
Piazza del Campo
Via del Porrione
PALAZZO PUBBLICO
Via di Città
Via di Salicotto
Via Dupré
PALAZZO PICCOLOMINI O DELLE PAPESSE
Via di Sotto
PALAZZO CHIGI-SARACINI
Via del Capitano
Via del Sole
Via San Pietro
Via Giovanni
Via Porta Giustizia
Via di Stalloreggi
Casato
Via Tito Sarrocchi

PALAZZO PUBBLICO Piazza del Campo.
This handsome red-brick town hall houses the Museo Civico (see SIENA-MUSEUMS*) and Torre del Mangia (1325-44). See* SIENA-ATTRACTIONS.

PALAZZO PICCOLOMINI Banchi di Sotto 52.
0930-1300 Mon.-Fri., 0900-1230 Sat. Free.
A Renaissance complex of buildings designed by Rossellino, containing the State archives, dating back to AD *736, and the famous medieval Biccherna illuminated registers.*

PALAZZO CHIGI-SARACINI Via di Città 89.
Apply to the music academy to view.
12th-14thC grey- and red-brick palace. Since 1932 it has housed the Accademia Musicale Chigiana. See 13th-15thC paintings and sculptures.

PALAZZO SANSEDONI Piazza del Campo.
Closed to the public.
A three-storey building (1219) with unusual curved tripartite windows.

PALAZZO PICCOLOMINI O DELLE PAPESSE Via di Città.
Closed to the public.
Built in 1460 by Rossellino for Pope Pius II's sister, Caterina.

PALAZZO TOLOMEI Piazza Tolomei 11.
Closed to the public.
Built 1207-65, this is the oldest family palazzo *in Siena.*

PIAZZA SALIMBENI Off Banchi di Sopra.
Three elegant 14thC palazzi *– Salimbeni, Tantucci and Spanocchi – now house the Mte dei Paschi di Siena, the oldest bank in Siena (1472).*

SANTUARIO E CASA DI SANTA CATERINA
Costa Sant'Antonio, Via Santa Caterina.
0900-1230, 1530-1800. Free.
14thC house of the Sienese saint, complete with a small museum about her, and gardens. See **St. Catherine of Siena**.

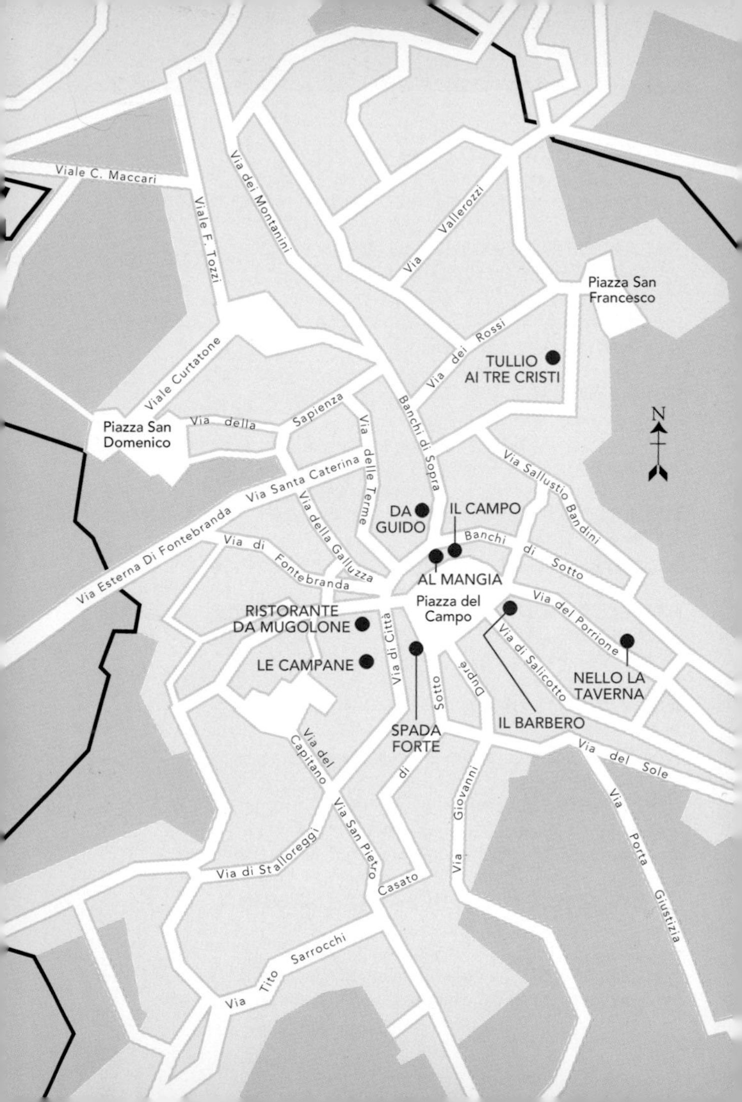
Viale C. Maccari
Viale F. Tozzi
Via dei Montanini
Via Vallerozzi
Piazza San Francesco
Via dei Rossi
TULLIO AI TRE CRISTI
Viale Curtatone
Piazza San Domenico
Via della Sapienza
Via delle Terme
Banchi di Sopra
N
Via Santa Caterina
Via Sallustio Bandini
Via Esterna Di Fontebranda
Via della Galluzza
DA GUIDO
IL CAMPO
Via di Fontebranda
Banchi di Sotto
AL MANGIA
Piazza del Campo
RISTORANTE DA MUGOLONE
Via di Città
Via del Porrione
LE CAMPANE
Via di Salicotto
NELLO LA TAVERNA
Dupré
Sotto
SPADA FORTE
IL BARBERO
Via del Capitano
Via del Sole
di
Via Giovanni
Via San Pietro
Via Porta Giustizia
Via di Stalloreggi
Casato
Via Tito Sarrocchi

IL CAMPO Piazza del Campo 50.
1230-1445, 1915-2130 Wed.-Mon. Expensive.
Try the cappelletti ai porcini *and* funghi di bosco e erbe aromatiche.

LE CAMPANE Vicolo delle Campane 4-6. 1200-1430, 1900-2100. Closed Sun. in season, Mon. out of season. Closed Nov. Expensive.
Classic Tuscan fish and meat cuisine and wines in a discreet setting.

DA GUIDO Vicolo B. Pier Pettinaio 7.
1200-1430, 1915-2130 Thu.-Tue. Expensive.
Perhaps the best restaurant in town. Try panforte *or* ricciarelli *as a sweet.*

NELLO LA TAVERNA Via del Porrione 28-32.
1215-1430 Tue.-Sun., 1930-2130 Tue.-Sat. Moderate-Expensive.
One of the top-ranking Sienese restaurants, serving traditional dishes. Don't be put off by the drab exterior.

AL MANGIA Piazza del Campo 42.
1215-1430, 1900-2145 Tue.-Sun. Closed Feb. Moderate-Expensive.
Try carpaccio ai radicchi e parmigiano *(beef with cheese and radishes).*

TULLIO AI TRE CRISTI Vicolo Provenzano 1-7.
1230-1430, 1930-2145 Tue.-Sun. Closed Jan. & Feb. Moderate.
Small restaurant, founded 1830, serving piatti storici *(traditional dishes).*

RISTORANTE DA MUGOLONE Via dei Pellegrini 8-12.
1215-1415, 1915-2115 Fri.-Wed. Moderate.
Small, characterful restaurant. Try the L.10,000 per bottle house wines.

IL BARBERO Piazza del Campo 79-81.
1200-1430, 1900-2200 Sun.-Fri. Inexpensive.
The largest self-service restaurant in Tuscany! Menu changes daily.

SPADA FORTE Piazza del Campo 12-14.
1200-1430, 1900-2200 Sun.-Fri. Inexpensive.
Has a tourist menu for L.27,000 plus many pizzeria dishes.

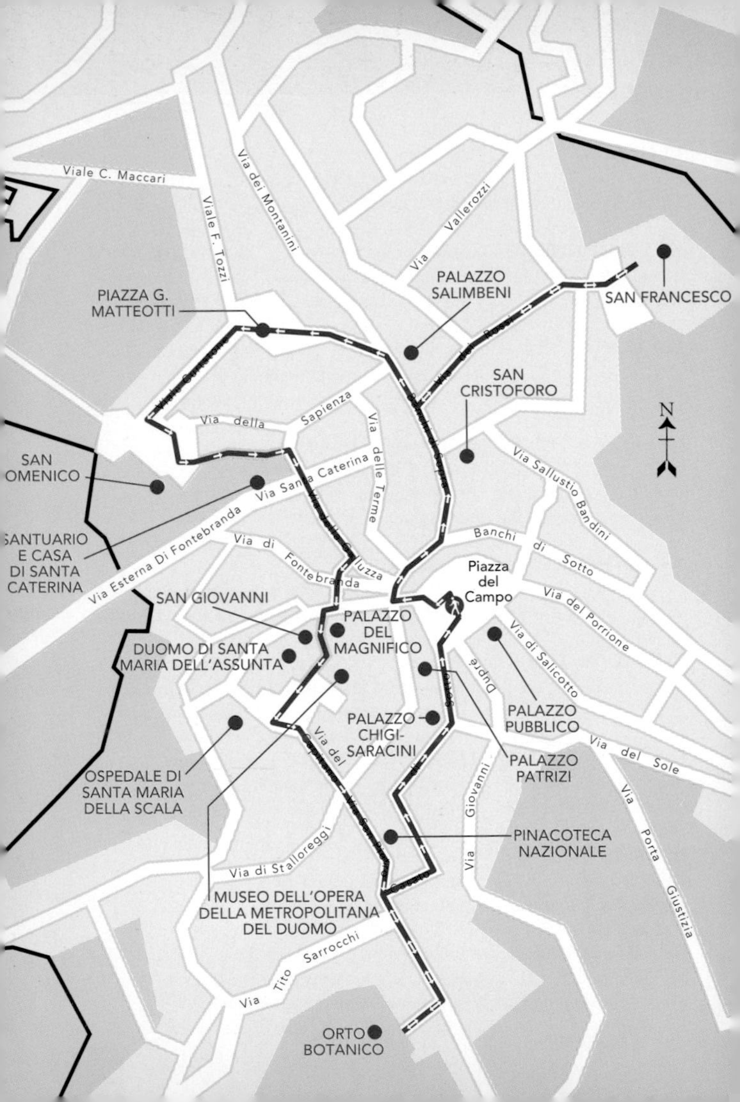

Viale C. Maccari
Viale F. Tozzi
Via dei Montanini
Via Vallerozzi
PALAZZO SALIMBENI
PIAZZA G. MATTEOTTI
SAN FRANCESCO
SAN CRISTOFORO
N
Via della
Sapienza
Via delle Terme
SAN
OMENICO
Via Santa Caterina
Via Sallustio Bandini
SANTUARIO E CASA DI SANTA CATERINA
Via Esterna Di Fontebranda
Via di Fontebranda
Banchi di Sotto
Piazza del Campo
Via del Porrione
SAN GIOVANNI
PALAZZO DEL MAGNIFICO
DUOMO DI SANTA MARIA DELL'ASSUNTA
Via di Salicotto
Dupre
PALAZZO PUBBLICO
PALAZZO CHIGI-SARACINI
PALAZZO PATRIZI
Via del Sole
OSPEDALE DI SANTA MARIA DELLA SCALA
Via Giovanni
Via Porta Giustizia
Via di Stalloreggi
PINACOTECA NAZIONALE
MUSEO DELL'OPERA DELLA METROPOLITANA DEL DUOMO
Via Tito Sarrocchi
ORTO BOTANICO

Duration: 3 hr, excluding visits.
Start at the tourist office in Piazza del Campo (see **SIENA-ATTRACTIONS**), having looked at the Palazzo Pubblico (see **SIENA-ATTRACTIONS, PALAZZI**), climbed the Torre del Mangia and toured the excellent Museo Civico (see **SIENA-MUSEUMS**). Turn right and right again into the long, narrow Via di Città, a smart street with *palazzi*, boutiques and restaurants. At the fork turn half-left along attractive Banchi di Sopra into little Piazza Tolomei (see **SIENA-PALAZZI**), with its fine *palazzi* occupied by competing banks, opposite the pink church of San Cristoforo. Keep east and on the right is Via dei Rossi. The 14th-17thC Basilica San Francesco (see **SIENA-ATTRACTIONS**) is at the end, complete with its Lorenzetti (see **A-Z**) frescoes. On the corner of Piazza Salimbeni (see **SIENA-PALAZZI**) is the 14thC palace of that name and the Nannini emporium, with *marrons glacés, panforte margherita* and macaroons for sale. Note the statue to Sallustio Bandini, a prominent Sienese. Next go half-left on Via Pianigiani through Costa dell'Incrociata. On the left is the Consorzio Agrario, a large artisan co-op selling local wines, olive oil, honey, etc. The huge, uninspiring Piazza G. Matteotti is ahead, with the post office to the right. Descend some steps on the opposite side into Viale Curtatone, past the police station, an Evangelist church and the Communist party HQ on the left. At the end in Piazza San Domenico stands the gigantic, red-brick Dominican church of the same name (see **SIENA-ATTRACTIONS**). The interior has Sodoma frescoes and brilliant modern stained-glass windows. Leaving the gardens on the right, turn downhill half-left on Via Camporegio and Vicolo del Campaccio past the elegant pilgrims' hospice, the Santuario e Casa di Santa Caterina (see **SIENA-PALAZZI**). Continue along Costa Sant'Antonio and uphill on Via della Galluzza, one of the most picturesque medieval streets in Siena. There are two good inexpensive little restaurants here: Bagoga at No. 26 and Gambassino at No. 10. Turn right on Via di Diacceto; after 30 m there is a lovely view of San Domenico and the valley. La Porcella Bianca sells elegant ceramic and porcelain objects. At the end of the street in the piazza is the Battistero San Giovanni (see **SIENA-ATTRACTIONS**) and the 16thC Palazzo del Magnifico. Walk up the wide staircase on the left through a large white-marble archway into the great Piazza del

Il Duomo

Duomo. Immediately on the left is the Museo dell'Opera della Metropolitana del Duomo (see **SIENA-MUSEUMS**), housed in the half-built remains of the Duomo Nuovo. On a corner is the yellow Palazzo della Prefettura, and opposite the cathedral is the Ospedale di Santa Maria della Scala (see **SIENA-ATTRACTIONS**), the third most important building, architecturally speaking, in Siena (after the Duomo and Palazzo Pubblico). Completed in 1215, Il Duomo di Santa Maria dell'Assunta (see **SIENA-ATTRACTIONS**) has a splendid façade in black, white, green and pink marble, great cupola, triangular mosaic, and a Romanesque campanile built in 1313. The marble floor inside has 56 designs produced by 40 Sienese artists, including some rather cross-looking sibyls and the badges of each town ward (*contrade*). See the great Piccolomini altar (1503), Pisano's (see **A-Z**) pulpit with statues by Michelangelo (see **A-Z**) and many animals carved at its foot, the high altar in the presbytery, the Chigi chapel and, off the left nave, the famous Libreria Piccolomini (see **SIENA-MUSEUMS**). You will need 1 hr or more to do justice to this superb church. When you leave, go down the steps, turn left in the wide Via del Capitano, with *palazzi* on both sides, to Piazza di Postierla. On the corner, Cantoni Pepi sells every Tuscan wine. Keep south on Via San Pietro towards the huge Pinacoteca Nazionale (see **SIENA-MUSEUMS**) in the graceful Palazzo Buonsignori. Four hundred metres further south, in Via Pier Andrea Mattioli, are the Orto Botanico (0800-1700 Mon.-Sat. am; Free, guided tours on weekdays), founded in 1784 and now a peaceful haven with hundreds of species of local and 'foreign' flora, and the church of Sant'Agostino. Turn right on Casato di Sopra, a long, winding, narrow, downhill street with *palazzi* and several restaurants. Occasional *vicoli* (alleyways) on the right give stunning views of campaniles on the skyline. Note the black-bronze wall statues of the 'nobil Contrada dell'Aquila' and at No. 89 the huge, five-storey, 13thC Palazzo Chigi-Saracini (see **SIENA-PALAZZI**), and a picture gallery. Piazza del Campo is 200 m further on.

Piazza del Campo, Siena

Abbeys: There are a number of beautiful abbeys and monasteries in the Tuscan countryside which are well worth a visit: the Carthusian monastery in Calci, 9 km east of Pisa; the medieval Abbadia Isola (see **SIENA-EXCURSION**), 18 km southeast of Siena; the 14thC red-brick abbey of Mte Oliveto Maggiore, 36 km southeast of Siena (see **AREZZO-EXCURSION**); the hill-top Carthusian monastery of Certosa del Galluzzo (see **FLORENCE-EXCURSION**), 9 km southwest of Florence; the Franciscan monastery of La Verna founded by St. Francis (see **A-Z**), 58 km north of Arezzo; Charlemagne's monastery of Sant'Antimo (see **AREZZO-EXCURSION**) founded in AD 813, 8 km south of Montalcino; the ruined 14thC Cistercian abbey of San Galgano, 35 km southwest of Siena; and the 11thC Monasterio di Camaldoli in the Apennines, 46 km north of Arezzo.

Angelico, Fra Giovanni (c.1400-55): Born Guido di Pietro in Fiesole, little is known of Angelico's artistic training but his deep piety led him to the Dominican order and his resultant output was religious in nature. He was one of the most celebrated and progressive artists of the Renaissance and many of his exquisitely coloured works can be seen in the Museo di San Marco (see **FLORENCE-MUSEUMS 2**) at San Marco monastery, the cells of which are decorated with his famous series of frescoes. More of his masterpieces can be seen in the Galleria degli Uffizi (see **FLORENCE-MUSEUMS 1**), the Monasterio di San Domenico (see **Fiesole**), Montecarlo monastery and the Museo Diocesano in Cortona (see **A-Z**).

Arezzo: 81 km southeast of Florence. Pop: 93,000. Tourist information: Piazza Risorgimento 116. This is the birthplace of Petrarch, Giorgio Vasari (see **A-Z**), Maecenas and Pietro Aretino (Piero della Francesca – see **A-Z** – was born in nearby Sansepolcro). Arezzo claims to have the best cuisine in Tuscany: the wine and olive oil (see **A-Z**) are certainly excellent. Gifts made of straw, metal, wood and gold plate, as well as costume jewellery, are all available. The frescoes of Piero della Francesca in the Chiesa di San Francesco, *The Legend of the True Cross* (1452-66), are one of the most important sights in Tuscany. Despite damage during World War II, the *centro storico*, with its old streets and delightful Piazza Grande, scene of a spectacular medieval joust (see **Events**), should be seen, as should Cosimo I's medieval Fortezza Medicea, Palazzo Comunale, Casa Petrarca and the public gardens in Passeggio del Prato. A well-known antique fair is held on the 1st Sun. of each month. See **AREZZO**.

Arno, Fiume: This mighty river rises on Mte Falterona, some 50 km east of Florence. However, it flows due south towards Arezzo, then west, then north for 80 km before its famous journey through the city. A trickle in summer, it is a dangerous muddy-brown torrent in midwinter, and flooded the city in 1966. The Arno continues west past Empoli, through Pisa and finally reaches the Mediterranean at the Marina di Pisa.

Bagni di Lucca: 27 km north of Lucca. Pop: 8000. Tourist information: Via Umberto 101. This was once a well-known spa town, frequented by the European gentry and their ladies in the 19thC, with 19 hot springs from the river Lima. Now the little town is run-down and the English cemetery neglected and forlorn. The springs and two steam vapour grottoes are open May-Sep.

Barga: 37 km north of Lucca. Pop: 8000. Tourist information: Piazza Angelico. A pretty, old town on a hillside, full of churches and monasteries (including the 9thC Duomo), which has an opera festival in July.

Baroque: A style which prevailed in the art and architecture of the 17thC and is characterized by an uninhibited use of elaborate decoration.

Boccaccio, Giovanni (1313-75): Born in Certaldo Alto, he lived alternately in Florence and Naples. A diplomat and poet, he is famous for his *Decameron* (1353) in which 10 refugees from the plague each tell 10 funny, licentious, poetic and sometimes serious stories.

Botticelli, Sandro (1444-1510): A pupil of Fra Filippo Lippi (see **A-Z**) and convert of the fiery monk Savonarola (see **A-Z**), this painter of allegorical, religious and mythological subjects is mainly known today for his portraits of women. The Galleria degli Uffizi (see **FLORENCE-MUSEUMS 1**) houses *Primavera* (Spring), *La Nascita di Venere* (Birth of Venus) and *Madonna of the Magnificat.*

Brunelleschi, Filippo (1377-1446): This goldsmith, architect and sculptor designed many Florentine churches, including Santo Spirito, San Lorenzo, the Cappella dei Pazzi and the cupola of the Duomo (1436) (see **FLORENCE-CHURCHES 1 & 2**). He was one of two architects of the Palazzo Pitti (see **FLORENCE-PALAZZI**) and two *palazzi* in Via Guelfa, Cortona.

Carrara: 55 km north of Pisa. Pop: 70,000. Tourist information: Piazza Guigno 14. The town has produced the famous marble (as used by Michelangelo – see **A-Z**) from its quarries for over 2000 years. From the autostrada you can see on the hillsides the quarries of Colonnata and Fantiscritti, which produce half a million tons of marble annually. If you brave the white, dusty and brash 'new' town you will find the marble-faced 12thC Duomo in the centre on the river Carrione. By contrast, the Mostra Nazionale di Marmi e Macchine (1000-1300 Mon. & Thu., 1000-1300, 1600-1900 Sun.; L.5000) in Viale XX Settembre is a permanent exhibition of marble-quarrying techniques.

Cellini, Benvenuto (1500-71): This Florentine sculptor, goldsmith, gunner and autobiographer worked for popes Clement VII and Paul III in Rome. He also worked in Paris and produced a golden salt cellar for King François I. A great admirer of Michelangelo (see **A-Z**), Cellini is remembered for his statue *Perseus slaying the Gorgon* in the Loggia dei Lanzi. The Museo Nazionale del Bargello (see **FLORENCE-**

Duomo, Florence

MUSEUMS 1) specializes in sculptures and Cellini's model for the *Perseus* can be seen there, as well as four bronze statues.

Cimabue, Giovanni (c. 1240-c. 1302): A Florentine painter and mosaicist much admired by Dante (see **A-Z**) and probably the teacher of Giotto (see **A-Z**), Cimabue is best-known for the mosaic in Il Duomo di Santa Maria Assunta (see **PISA-ATTRACTIONS**), his *Crucifixion* in the Museo Cimabue (see **FLORENCE-MUSEUMS 2**) and the *Santa Trinità Madonna* in the Galleria degli Uffizi (see **FLORENCE-MUSEUMS 1**).

Cortona: 32 km southeast of Arezzo. Pop: 22,500. Tourist information: Piazza Signorelli 10. This old Etruscan hill town on the border with Umbria is rather off the beaten track. The medieval brown sandstone buildings and town walls cluster together on the slopes of Mte Sant'Egidio. The Piazza della Repubblica and Piazza del Duomo at the west end of the town should be visited to see the 10thC Duomo di Santa Maria, and the Museo Diocesano (0900-1300, 1500-1800 Tue.-Sun.; L.5000) in the 16thC church of Gesù, with fine paintings by Fra Angelico (see **A-Z**), Duccio and Sassetta. Cortona itself produced several notable painters, including Signorelli (see **A-Z**), Pietro da Cortona and Gino Severini, whose works can also be seen in the museum. The Museo Etrusco (1000-1300, 1600-1800 Tue.-Sun.; L.5000, free Thu.) is in the 13thC Palazzo Pretorio in Piazza Signorelli. Note the intriguing mural of governors' escutcheons and see the excellent collection of 5thC Etruscan and Roman bronze statues, jewellery, ceramics, oil lamps and candelabra. There are a dozen 13th-15thC *palazzi* within a few minutes' walk of Piazza della Repubblica, and the Fortezza Medicea, built in 1549 by Laparelli, has superb views across the Tuscan hills and plains. The Hotel St. Luca, with the Tonino restaurant on the ramparts, in Piazza Garibaldi, provides excellent meals. See **AREZZO-EXCURSION**.

Dante Alighieri (1265-1321): Italy's greatest poet was a native of Florence but was exiled in 1302 because of his political activities. He died in Ravenna after writing his *Divine Comedy*, the visionary masterpiece of hell, purgatory and heaven. See Michelino's painting *Dante declaiming the Divine Comedy* in the Florence Duomo (see **FLORENCE-CHURCHES 1**), where Dante was baptized. By contrast, *La Vita Nuova* recounts Dante's profound Platonic love for Beatrice Portinari, aged 9 when he met her. The house on the corner of Via Dante Alighieri and Via Santa Margherita where Dante lived can also be visited (see **FLORENCE-WALK**).

Elba: Pop: 29,000. Tourist information: Calata Italia 26, Portoferraio. The largest of the Tuscan islands, 27 km long and 18 km at its widest, this tropical and mountainous island – made famous by Napoleon's exile – is surrounded by turquoise sea, and host to a million visitors every Aug., so try to plan your visit for the spring or autumn. The *traghetto* (car ferry) from mainland Piombino to Portoferraio, Elba's largest town (pop: 11,000), takes 1 hr (the hydrofoil takes 30 min) and costs approximately L.6000 per person for a one-way ticket. The 'Freccia d'Elba' train leaves Florence at approximately 0630 to connect with the ferry or hydrofoil and passengers reach Elba 4 hr later. Daily flights from Pisa land at the airport near Marina di Campo. The round tour of the island takes about 5 hr, either by rented car (Avis, Arrighi, etc.), by ACIT bus or rented moped/bicycle. The two main sights are Napoleon's houses, Villa dei Mulini and Villa di San Martino (0900-1330 Tue.-Sat., 0900-1230 Sun.; combined ticket L.4000). The emperor spent nearly a year on the island during 1814-15, before his dramatic return to the mainland, the hundred days, Waterloo and his exile to St. Helena. There are many sandy beaches, including Procchio, Lacona and Marciana Marina, and 50 little coves reached by boat. The water is clear, the swimming superb and views incomparable. A cable car (1000-1200, 1430-1800; L.15,000) from Marciana will take you up Mte Capanne. From the top at 1089 m you can see the whole island and mainland Italy. There are 140 hotels on Elba and the many restaurants in the seven small towns all serve locally-caught fish and reasonable local wines (*aleatico*) grown near Marciana. Excursions can be made by boat to the island of Capraia which takes 2.5 hr, and by arrangement to the island of Montecristo, an uninhabited nature reserve (see **A-Z**).

Fiesole

Empoli: 33 km west of Florence. Pop: 46,000. Tourist information: Piazza Farinata degli Uberti. In this rather unattractive town is the collegiate church of Sant'Andrea in Piazza Farinata degli Uberti. With its white and green marble stripes, it dates from 1093. The Museo della Collegiata (1000-1200 Tue.-Sun.) in nearby Piazzetta San Giovanni has a notable collection of sacred art with works by the local painters Pontormo and Chimenti. Vasari's (see **A-Z**) 16thC frescoes of Empoli can be seen in Palazzo Vecchio (see **FLORENCE-PALAZZI**), showing it as a fortified town before it was badly damaged by bombs in World War II.

Etruscan Civilization: From the 8th-4thC BC the Etruscans, oldest of the local Italian tribes, occupied the region of Etruria. Seafarers, traders and skilled craftsmen, their rule extended to Naples in the south and the Po valley in the north. But in 351 BC, the Romans annexed Etruria. Fortunately, many Etruscan necropolises (tombs, grottoes and frescoes) have survived in the south of Tuscany at Grosseto (see **A-Z**), Cosa, Sovana, Vulci and Tarquinia. Populonia, 15 km north of Plombino, is the only surviving Etruscan town built on a coastal site. There are a small Etruscan museum and necropolis 3 km east of the village. The main museums housing rare Etruscan finds are in Florence (see **FLORENCE-MUSEUMS 2**), Chiusi (see **AREZZO-EXCURSION**) and Volterra (see **A-Z**).

Fiesole: 8 km northeast of Florence. Pop: 15,000. Tourist information: Piazza Mino da Fiesole 45. An important Etruscan hill town, Fiesole's attractive wooded landscape attracted the Medicis (see **A-Z**), Boccaccio (see **A-Z**), and later Shelley and Dickens. It is an essential visit from Florence (Bus 7) to see the 11th-14thC Duomo di San Romolo in Piazza Mino da Fiesole, and the Monasterio di San Francesco in Via San Francesco on a steep hill above the public gardens – once a fortress, then a convent, now a Franciscan monastery at one time used by St. Bernardino of Siena (see **A-Z**). From the top there are superb views over Florence and the Arno (see **A-Z**) valley. Note the beautiful courtyards and eclectic oriental museum beneath the 15thC cloister in the Capuchin convent (1000-1230, 1500-1800; Donation). The Museo Bandini (1000-1300, 1500-1900 Wed.-Mon.; L.3000) at Via Dupré 18, behind the Duomo, has della Robbia (see **A-Z**) terracottas and works by Gaddi, T. Daddi, Bicci di Lorenzo and other masters of the 14th-15thC, collected by Canon Bandini. Fiesole has a significant Roman complex, with a well-preserved theatre dating back to c. 80 BC (used for the Estate Fiesolana festival of music, drama and film in June and July), ruins of a Roman temple and baths, and a small archaeological museum, the Museo Romano-Scavi (0900-1300, 1500-1900 Tue.-Sun.; L.5000), on Via Marini next to the Duomo. There are also two notable sights on the Florence–Fiesole road. Three kilometres south is the 11thC Badia Fiesolana, once the cathedral but now home of the European University, which is open to view the paintings and cloisters (free). The 15th-17thC Monasterio di San Domenico (0700-1230, 1500-1930; Free) is 2.5 km southwest and has works by Fra Angelico (see **A-Z**), Jacopo da Empoli and Lorenzo di Credo.

Florence: Firenze. 277 km north of Rome. Pop: 460,000. Tourist information: Azienda di Promozione Turistica Firenze, Via Manzoni 16, tel: 055-2478141; Chiasso Baroncelli 17-19r, tel: 055-2302124; near the Galleria degli Uffizi (general information and town map); and at the station (hotel bookings).
The capital of Tuscany is bisected by the river Arno (see **A-Z**) and lies in the heart of Italy. Florentine bankers were trading in London in 1199, and in the next century they issued bills of exchange and funded Edward III at the beginning of the Hundred Years' War. Powerful, able and talented families such as the Pittis, Strozzis and, above all, the Medicis (see **A-Z**), ensured Florence's fame and prosperity, which reached its zenith in the 14thC with Dante Alighieri (see **A-Z**), Petrarch and Boccaccio (see **A-Z**). Florentine Renaissance (see **A-Z**) painters included Giotto (see **A-Z**), Masaccio (see **A-Z**), Fra Angelico (see **A-Z**), Fra Filippo Lippi (see **A-Z**), Botticelli (see **A-Z**) and Michelangelo (see **A-Z**) – the greatest assembly of talent in the world. Great sculptors included Ghiberti (see **A-Z**), Donatello, Luca della Robbia (see **A-Z**) and Cellini (see **A-Z**). Little wonder that every traveller on the Grand Tour had to visit Florence. Even now, over four centuries later, there are 400 palaces, 50 churches and 22 museums (the Uffizi, Pitti and Accademia ranking among the greatest in the world).

The city is such a powerhouse of art that a minimum stay of three days is suggested, with perhaps alternate visits to museums/art galleries and churches. Florence is always crowded with tourists, so planning is important, particularly as there is little alternative to walking. However, a long one-day visit could take in the Duomo, Giotto's Campanile and Battistero, a walk to see the Palazzo Vecchio, the Galleria degli Uffizi, then across the river Arno (see **A-Z**) and Ponte Vecchio to the Palazzo Pitti and a rest in the Boboli gardens. The shopping temptations are immense – leatherware, gold jewellery, shoes, lingerie – but fortunately for the exhausted sightseer, there are also dozens of restaurants serving dishes *alla fiorentina*. See **FLORENCE**.

Francis, St. of Assisi (c. 1181-1226): On 14 Sep. 1224 Francis of Assisi is thought to have received the stigmata while praying on the wooded slopes of Mte Penna at La Verna, 58 km north of Arezzo. He founded Le Celle convent, 3.5 km northeast of Cortona, where his cell can be visited, and the monastery of La Verna (see **Abbeys**), which is still a centre for pilgrimages on 17 Sep. and 4 Oct.

Galileo Galilei (1564-1642): The Pisa-born astronomer, physicist and philosopher became court mathematician to Cosimo II in Florence in 1610. There he invented the telescope and detected the moons of Jupiter, mountains on the moon and many stars. As a young man of 25 he demonstrated the first principles of dynamics at Pisa, where he taught at the university. He is believed to have dropped three metal balls of different masses from the Torre Pendente (see **PISA-ATTRACTIONS**) to disprove Aristotle's theories about the acceleration of falling bodies. His treatises include *Dialogue concerning the Two Chief World Systems* and *The Two New Sciences*. He is buried in Santa Croce (see **FLORENCE-CHURCHES 1**).

Ghiberti, Lorenzo (1378-1455): A Renaissance sculptor, architect, goldsmith, painter and writer, he spent 22 years sculpting the exquisitely beautiful *Porta del Paradiso* bronze doors of the Florence Battistero (see **FLORENCE-CHURCHES 1**). He is buried close to Galileo (see **A-Z**) in Santa Croce (see **FLORENCE-CHURCHES 1**).

Ghirlandaio, Domenico (1449-94): Ghirlandaio was a teacher of Michelangelo (see **A-Z**) and painted religious frescoes which depicted the local citizens. *The Life of St. John the Baptist* in the church of Santa Maria Novella (see **FLORENCE-CHURCHES 1**) documents Ghirlandaio's own contemporary social history. His cycle of frescoes on Mary's life is also in Santa Maria Novella, and *The Last Supper* is in the San Marco church.
Other frescoes can be seen in the Santa Fina chapel of the Duomo, and his *Annunciation* in the baptistry loggia, both in San Gimignano (see **A-Z**). His brother Davide and son Ridolfo continued the family painting tradition.

Giglio: 14 km southeast of Mte Argentario. Pop: 1800. The second-largest island in the Tuscan archipelago, at 8 km long and 5 km wide, Giglio is reached by sea from Porto Santo Stefano (1 hr). There are three good beaches, the hotels Arenella and Il Saraceno, and several restaurants.

Giotto di Bondone (c.1267-1337): A pupil of Cimabue (see **A-Z**), this painter and architect lived at Vespignano near Florence, where in 1334 he was appointed Master of Works of the Duomo. He also painted frescoes for four chapels in Santa Croce (see **FLORENCE-CHURCHES 1**) and designed the multi-coloured Campanile (see **FLORENCE-CHURCHES 1**) for the Duomo. In Padua he painted the Arena chapel, and in Assisi the frescoes in San Francesco. His *Ognissanti Madonna* is in the Galleria degli Uffizi (see **FLORENCE-MUSEUMS 1**).

Gothic: A style of European architecture prevalent in the 12th-16thC characterized by narrow pillars, pointed arches and high vaults.

Grosseto: 73 km south of Siena. Pop: 70,000. Tourist information: Viale Monterosa 206. The capital of the Tuscan Maremma region, the flat coastal plain which has ten resorts, Etruscan necropolises and several nature parks suitable for horse riding, bird-watching, canoeing and walking.
Heavily bombed during World War II, this modern city still has the 14thC Duomo di San Lorenzo in Piazza Dante, the 13thC church of San Francesco and the Museo Archeologico e d'Arte della Maremma (0930-1230, 1630-1900 Thu.-Tue.; L.5000) at Piazza Baccarini 3, which has a good collection of Etruscan and Roman artefacts, and 13th-17thC Sienese paintings. Restaurants include La Maremma (closed Tue.) and Enoteca Ombrone, which has a stock of 40 varieties of olive oil and a good wine cellar. Grosseto is an ideal base for excursions to Castiglione della Pescaia and other resorts to the west; the Parco Naturale della Maremma (see **Nature Reserves**); Orbetello, Porto Ercole (see **A-Z**) and the 'island' of Mte Argentario to the south; and Etruscan necropolises to the east and southeast.

Hawkwood, Sir John: This famous 14thC British condottiere (i.e. mercenary) was Captain General of Florence (1375-90). He was hired by the city in 1384 to capture Arezzo, and was given the 13thC hill-top Castello di Montecchio Vesponi, just south of Arezzo, as a reward. See the three-dimensional monument to him by Paolo Uccello in the Duomo (see **FLORENCE-CHURCHES 1**).

za della Signoria, Florence

Leonardo da Vinci (1452-1519): Born in Vinci, north of Empoli, Leonardo was a painter, sculptor, architect, engineer, anatomist, author, man of science and philosopher! Although *The Last Supper* (1498) is in Milan, *Virgin of the Rocks* in London and the *Mona Lisa* (1504) in the Louvre, three paintings remain in Tuscany, all in the Galleria degli Uffizi (see **FLORENCE-MUSEUMS 1**): *The Adoration of the Magi* (1480), *The Annunciation* (1475) and *Baptism of Christ* (1470) can be seen in Room 15. Leonardo moved to Milan in 1482, Florence in 1502, returned to Milan in 1506 and died in Amboise, France in 1519. The medieval castle of the Conti Guidi in Vinci houses the Museo Vinciano and Biblioteca Leonardiana (both 0930-1200, 1500-1800; L.4000) which have a large selection of mechanical models and documentation on his life.

Lippi, Filippino (c. 1457-1504): Son of Filippo (see below) and pupil of Botticelli (see **A-Z**), he painted important frescoes in Florence and Rome, and completed Masaccio (see **A-Z**) and Masolino's frescoes in the chapel of Santa Maria del Carmine (see **FLORENCE-CHURCHES 2**). Also see his *St. Bernard's Vision of the Madonna* in the Badia Fiorentina (see **FLORENCE-CHURCHES 2**), the lives of SS Philip and John in the Strozzi chapel of Santa Maria Novella (see **FLORENCE-CHURCHES 1**), frescoes in the same church, and works in the church of San Frediano.

Lippi, Fra Filippo (c.1406-69): Ordained at 15, he fled his monastery, was sold as a slave in Africa and returned to Prato where he married a nun, Lucrezia Buti, whose face he used as a model for his Madonnas and Salomes. Note his frescoes of the lives of SS Stephen and John the Baptist in Prato Duomo (see **PRATO-ATTRACTIONS**), works in Palazzo Corsi (see **FLORENCE-PALAZZI**), his *Madonna and Child* (1452) in Palazzo Pitti (see **FLORENCE-MUSEUMS 1**), *Annunciation* in San Lorenzo church (see **FLORENCE-CHURCHES 1**) and *Madonna with Angels* (c. 1465) in the Galleria degli Uffizi (see **FLORENCE-MUSEUMS 1**).

Livorno: Leghorn. 19 km south of Pisa. Pop: 177,000. Tourist information: Piazza Cavour. This major commercial port created by the

Medici (see **A-Z**) grand dukes was partly constructed in 1621 by Robert Dudley, a marine engineer in their service. Of interest are the two 16thC fortresses which guard the harbour, the statue of Ferdinand I (1595), the English cemetery at Via Verdi 63, the Museo Civico (1000-1300, 1700-2000 Tue.-Sat.; L.4000) in Villa Fabricotti, with Italian 15th-17thC paintings, and the 1594 Duomo of San Francisco d'Assisi in Piazza Grande. Many excellent fish restaurants cluster around the old port, from where ferries sail to Elba (see **A-Z**), Corsica and Sardinia.

Lorenzetti, Ambrogio & Pietro: These 14thC Sienese brothers created the first known European landscape painting, *Città sul Mare*. Pietro's great fresco *Good and Bad Government*, is in the Palazzo Pubblico at Siena (see **SIENA-ATTRACTIONS**), and other works can be seen in Arezzo, Cortona and Siena.

Lucca: 22 km northeast of Pisa. Pop 92,000. Tourist information: Via Vittorio Veneto 40. The old town behind the plane tree-shaded ramparts, built 1544-1645, remains a medieval city state with tall red houses, towers, 16thC *palazzi*, church spires and narrow streets. Once a great banking and silk trade centre, owing much to Napoleon Bonaparte's sister, Elisa, Lucca has preserved its character supremely well. Throughout the year there are musical events, with opera at the Teatro Comunale del Giglio (see **Music**). Lucca is well known for its olive oil (see **A-Z**), wine, flowers and textiles, and is an essential visit. In particular, see the venerated *Volto Santo*, the Holy Countenance referred to in Dante's *Inferno*, kept in a small marble temple in the Duomo. See **LUCCA**.

Machiavelli, Niccolò (1469-1527): This Florentine statesman and political theorist held office in the Medici (see **A-Z**) administration for many years. Dismissed in 1512, he went to Sant'Andrea in Percussina outside Florence. His work *The Prince* (1513), a treatise on Renaissance statesmanship, is typically cynical and amoral, i.e. 'The end justifies the means.' His tomb is in Santa Croce (see **FLORENCE-CHURCHES 1**).

Masaccio (1401-28): The founder of Florentine Renaissance painting. See *The Tribute Money* frescoes in Santa Maria del Carmine (see **FLORENCE-CHURCHES 2**) and his *Trinity* in Santa Maria Novella (see **FLORENCE-CHURCHES 1**). His work influenced Leonardo da Vinci (see **A-Z**), Botticelli (see **A-Z**) and Michelangelo (see **A-Z**).

Massa: 45 km northeast of Pisa. Pop: 66,000. An unattractive marble-producing town redeemed by its interesting medieval centre which contains the 13thC Duomo (the crypt is a museum), and is dominated by its formidable fortress, now a cultural centre (0900-1200, 1600-1900). The 17thC Palazzo Cybo Malaspina and courtyard, and Piazza degli Aranci are also worth a look.

Massa Marittima: 64 km southwest of Siena. Pop: 10,300. Tourist information: Palazzo Comunale, Piazza Garibaldi. The Città Vecchia, the Romanesque lower walled town (1228-1304), contains Palazzo Comunale, Palazzo Pretorio and the Duomo di San Cerbone. The Città Nuova is the upper town built in Gothic style, enclosing within its walls the Fortezza dei Senesi (1837), a massive fort with tall towers and arches. Other sights include the 13thC church of Sant'Agostino and two museums: the Museo Archeologico e Civico (1000-1200, 1400-1800 Mon.-Sat., 1000-1200 Sun., April-Oct.; L.4000) in Palazzo delle Armi, Corso A. Diaz, with Etruscan urns, vases and majolica; and the Museo di Mineralogia e Miniera (1000-1200, 1400-1800 Mon.-Sat.; L.4000) in Viale Martiri di Niccoletta, depicting the history of copper, silver and iron-ore mining, for which Massa Marittima has been famous for 1000 years. A joint ticket is available for both museums. Trattoria Roma at Via Parenti 19 serves guinea fowl and wild boar, and is recommended.

Medici: This great Florentine family of merchants and bankers held official power in the city from 1464 until the 18thC. Among the most famous members of the dynasty, which provided Italy and western Europe with popes, patrons and rulers, were Cosimo the Elder (1389-1464), who unofficially ruled Florence for over 30 years, his grandson Lorenzo the Magnificent (1449-92), who was a great patron of the arts and brilliant politician (Florence became the intellectual and artistic capital of Europe under his leadership), and Lorenzo II de' Medici (1492-1519), father of Catherine de' Medici who became a queen of France (as did Maria, Cosimo I's granddaughter). Popes Leo X (1475-1521) and Clement VII (1478-1534) also belonged to this illustrious family. See **Medici Villas**.

Medici Villas: Around Florence are a number of important 14th-16thC villas or castles built for the great Medici (see **A-Z**) princes and cardinals. These include the 14thC castle and gardens of Villa Medicea della Petraia (0900-1400 Tue.-Sat.; Free); Villa Medicea di Careggi (now a nursing home); and Villa Medicea di Castello (0900-1830; grotto and gardens only, free). All three are near Castello, 6 km northwest of Florence. Two more are at Trebbio (closed to the public) and Cafaggiolo (now a hospital), while Villa Medicea di Poggio a Caiano (0830-1830, gardens only), built for Lorenzo de' Medici in 1480, and Villa del'Artimino (now a restaurant) are respectively 17 km and 22 km west of the city. There are also two villas near Lucca; the Villa Reale at Marlia and the 16thC Villa Torrigiani.

Michelangelo Buonarroti (1475-1564): A painter, architect, draftsman, poet and sculptor who, with Leonardo da Vinci (see **A-Z**), is regarded as the greatest genius of the Renaissance (see **A-Z**). He spent his life in Florence working for the Medicis (see **A-Z**) and in Rome under Pope Julius II's patronage. His work in Florence dates from 1501: *David* in the Accademia (see **FLORENCE-MUSEUMS 1**), the *Pietà* in the Duomo (see **FLORENCE-CHURCHES 1**), the Medici tombs in San Lorenzo (see **FLORENCE-CHURCHES 1**) and the *Bacchus* in the Museo Nazionale del Bargello (see **FLORENCE-MUSEUMS 1**). He was born in Caprese, near Arezzo, and is buried in Santa Croce (see **FLORENCE-CHURCHES 1**). The Museo Michelangelo (see **FLORENCE-MUSEUMS 2**) has a fine collection of the master's drawings and sculptures.

Montalcino: 41 km south of Siena. Pop: 6000. Tourist information: Via Mazzini 33. Surprisingly, tourism has a low priority in this interesting medieval hill-top village. The massive 14thC fortress (0900-1300, 1400-1800; keep free, ramparts L.2000) dominating the town, the church of Sant'Edigio, and the Museo Civico e Diocesano (0930-1530 Tue.-Sun.; L.3000) at Via Spagni 4 all have a sad, neglected look about them. The Benedictine abbey of Sant'Antimo (see **Abbeys**) is 8 km to the south. See **AREZZO-EXCURSION**.

Montecatini Terme: 46 km northwest of Florence. Pop: 22,000. Tourist information: Viale Verdi 66. One of the most famous spas in Europe. The medieval fortified town is on the hill, and reached by road or funicular railway. The warm saline waters from nine established spas are recommended for gall bladder, stomach, liver and skin problems. There are 500 hotels which are usually open April-Nov., and many are clustered around the large Parco delle Terme. The best is the Grand Hotel e la Pace, Via della Torrenta 1, and two good restaurants are the Vittoria, Viale della Libertà 2, and Enoteca da Giovanni, Via Garibaldi 25. The Accademia d'Arte (1600-1900 Tue.-Sat.; L.5000) in Viale A. Diaz is a small modern-art museum.

Montepulciano: 65 km southeast of Siena. Pop: 14,300. Tourist information: Via Cavour 15. No cars are allowed in the town 0700-2000. This incomparable hill town has 15thC streets, churches and ten fine *palazzi*, including the Comunale, Contucci and Tarugi. Via Gracciano nel Corso and Via di Voltaia nel Corso lead up the hillside to the splendid Piazza Grande with its large gloomy 16thC Duomo, which has gold triptych altarpieces, and skull-and-crossboned tombs inlaid in the floor. The main façade has, surprisingly, no marble facing. The Museo Civico (0900-1300, 1700-1900 Tue.-Sun.; L.3500) in Via Ricci II is in Palazzo Neri-Orselli and houses 13th-17thC paintings, terracottas and 15thC illuminated manuscripts. In the first two weeks of Aug. the popular Cantiere Internazionale d'Arte takes place with 20thC music and opera being performed in the Teatro Poliziano (named after the 15thC scholar-poet who tutored the Medici – see **A-Z** – children). Vino Nobile di Montepulciano is one of the finest Tuscan wines (see **A-Z**) and there are several cantinas where you can taste and buy. The Hotel-Restaurant Il Marzocco in Piazza Savonarola is clean, modest and friendly. See **AREZZO-EXCURSION**.

Olive Oil: Tuscan olive oil is famous for its quality, flavour and texture. Each town claims its is the best! The harvest begins in Nov. or Dec. and is picked by hand, with plastic nets laid on the ground to catch the fruit. The fruit is then pressed at a local mill, traditionally by stone but more usually now by steel rollers. The acid content is vital.

The finest extra virgin has an acid level below 1%, followed by *soprafino, fino* and virgin olive oil. It goes rancid quickly and should be used within a year of pressing.

Pescia: 19 km northeast of Lucca. Pop: 19,000. Tourist information: Palazzo Comunale, Piazza Mazzini. Cut by the river Pescia, this pleasant horticultural town has its religious centre on the left bank around Piazza del Duomo and its civic centre on the right bank around Piazza Mazzini. There are a number of 13th-14thC churches and *palazzi,* and the good Museo Civico (1600-1900 Mon., Wed. & Fri.; L.3000) in Piazza San Stefano. The Ristorante Cacco at Viale Forti 84 (closed Mon. and midwinter) offers locally-grown *asparagi giganti.*

Pienza: 52 km southeast of Siena. Pop: 2700. Tourist information: Vicolo della Canonica 1. Pope Pius II was born here and commissioned the architect Rossellini to rebuild the original village of Corsignano in 1459. As a result Pienza is a classic Gothic/Renaissance small town well worth a visit to see the Piazza Pio II, Duomo Santa Maria Assunta, Palazzo Piccolomini (Bishop's Palace), Casa dei Canonici and Museo dell'Arte Sacra (1000-1300, 1500-1800; L.3000). The restaurant Il Prato at Piazza Dante 25 (closed Wed. and July) has good food and *vinsanto.* See **AREZZO-EXCURSION**.

Piero della Francesca (1420-92): A superb Renaissance painter and theoretician. His main works are *La Leggenda della Croce* (Legend of the True Cross) frescoes in the Chiesa di San Francesco in Arezzo (see **AREZZO-ATTRACTIONS**); the magnificent fresco of the *Magdalene* in the Arezzo Duomo (see **AREZZO-ATTRACTIONS**); *Battista Sforza* and *Federigo da Montefeltro* in the Galleria degli Uffizi (see **FLORENCE-MUSEUMS 1**); *Resurrection* and the polyptych *Madonna della Misericordia* in the Museo Civico, Sansepolcro (see **A-Z**); and the *Flagellation of Christ* in Urbino.

Pisa: 91 km west of Florence. Pop: 105,000. Tourist information: Piazza del Duomo and Lungarno Mediceo. Fortunately, the four 12thC gleaming white buildings on their grass platform, famous around the world, have survived all wars including World War II (which damaged Pisa quite badly). The Torre Pendente (Leaning Tower), Duomo della Santa Maria Assunta, Battistero and Camposanto Vecchio are miracles of religious art, besieged throughout the year by thousands of tourists. All English travellers on the Grand Tour had to visit Pisa, and W. S. Landor, Shelley, Byron and the Brownings lived here for short periods. Galileo (see **A-Z**) taught at the university, which for centuries has had a strong science faculty. You will need several hours to see Pisa's sights, including the Ponte di Mezzo, the old bridge over the river Arno (see

Santa Maria della Spina

A-Z), which gives a good view of the scores of elegant *palazzi* lining the river, and the beautiful little Chiesa Santa Maria della Spina, built in 1325. Pisa has many good hotels, including the Cavalieri, D'Azeglio and Grand Hotel Duomo, and makes an excellent base for excursions north to Lucca and Viareggio, or south to Livorno and Siena. See **PISA**.

Pisano, Andrea (1290-c. 1348): A sculptor, goldsmith and architect whose main works are the bronze doors for the Florence Battistero and reliefs for the Campanile (see **FLORENCE-CHURCHES 1**). His father Nicola and brother Giovanni produced superb pulpits for churches in Pisa, Siena and Pistoia.

Pistoia: 37 km northwest of Florence. Pop: 95,000. Tourist information: Palazzo del Vescovi, Piazza del Duomo. For centuries the citizens of Pistoia were known for their violence and rude manners. Their 16thC daggers were known as *pistolese*. When the first pistols were made they were so named because of the town's reputation. Around Piazza del Duomo are the Duomo di San Zeno with its 67 m-high campanile, 13thC frescoes, huge crypt and famous silver altar; the 14thC octagonal baptistry; the Bishop's Palace (now a bank); Palazzo

Ospedale del Ceppo

del Comune (town hall); and Palazzo Pretorio (law courts). Other churches of note are Sant'Andrea, dei Tau and San Giovanna Fuorcivitas. Note too, the startling frieze over the main door of the Ospedale del Ceppo. There are three museums: Museo Civico (0900-1300, 1500-1900 Tue.-Sat., 0900-1300 Sun.; L.4000) in Palazzo del Comune; Museo di San Zeno (guided tours 1000, 1130, 1530 Tue., Thu. & Fri.; L.3000) in Palazzo del Vescovi; and Museo Centro Marini (0900-1300, 1500-1900 Tue.-Sun.; Free) in Corso Gramsci. If Florence is 'full', Pistoia is a viable alternative. Communications by rail, road and bus are good, and hotel prices are cheaper. Recommended restaurants include Chiavi d'Oro, La Casa degli Amici and Rafanelli. The town serves as an ideal base for excursions to Prato, Montecatini Terme and Lucca.

Porto Ercole: 50 km south of Grosseto. Pop: 3400. Tourist information: Corso Italia 121. A smart and fashionable sailing resort on Mte Argentario 'island', guarded by three medieval fortresses. Ferries sail south to the island of Giannutri. The hotel-restaurants Il Pellicano and Don Pedro are attractive bases from which to explore southeast Tuscany.

Prato: 19 km northwest of Florence. Pop: 157,000. Tourist information: Via L. Muzzi 51. In the heart of this large, rich, bustling textile town lies a medieval centre within 13thC walls. Piazza del Duomo has in one corner the Gothic green and white striped Duomo di Santo Stefano which contains Filippo Lippi's (see **A-Z**) important *John the Baptist* and *Salome* frescoes, and also the revered Sacred Girdle (*Sacro Cingolo*) given by the Virgin to doubting Apostle Thomas. On 1 May, 15 Aug. and 16 Sep. it is displayed to enthusiastic crowds from Donatello and Michelozzo's pulpit. See also the Museo dell'Opera del Duomo, the massive 13thC Palazzo Pretorio, the municipal museum covered with shields and griffins in Piazza

del Comune, and Frederick II's Castello dell'Imperatore. Hotels in Prato are relatively inexpensive, and there are a number of good restaurants, including Baghino at Via dell'Accademia 9 and Da Francesco in Via Cambioni. See **PRATO**.

Puccini, Giacomo (1858-1924): The composer of operas settled near Lake Massaciuccoli, 16 km north of Pisa, in 1891, built a house and lived there until his death in 1924. Villa Puccini (0900-1200, 1500-1900; L.4500) is a shrine to his memory and includes his mausoleum. He wrote all his operas here except *Turandot*, and a music festival of his operas is held each Aug. in Torre del Lago Puccini. His birthplace in Via di Poggio, Lucca, is also a museum (see **LUCCA-ATTRACTIONS**) and contains records, photographs and his Steinway piano.

Renaissance: Florence was the centre of the Renaissance, the *Rinascita* or 'rebirth of art' in the 14thC, as defined in 1550 by Giorgio Vasari (see **A-Z**). This outburst of creative painting, architecture and literature was started by Giotto (see **A-Z**), Masaccio (see **A-Z**), Botticelli (see **A-Z**), Michelangelo (see **A-Z**) and Leonardo da Vinci (see **A-Z**). Encouraged by guilds, patrons and the Medici (see **A-Z**), canvases, frescoes, mosaics, sculptures and metal- and woodworking appeared from the studios of Florentine artists during the trecento (1300s), quattrocento (1400s) and cinquecento (1500s).

Robbia, Luca della (c. 1400-82): A sculptor famous for his glazed terracotta reliefs, mainly white Madonnas on a blue background. His sons Giovanni, Girolamo and nephew Andrea continued their elder's work. Their contributions can be seen in the Museo Nazionale del Bargello (see **FLORENCE-MUSEUMS 1**), the Duomo at Pistoia (see **A-Z**) and Mte Oliveto Maggiore abbey (see **Abbeys**).

Romanesque: A style of European architecture which prevailed in the 11th-12thC and is characterized by vaulted churches decorated outside with marble bands, round arches, massive walls and separate campaniles (bell towers).

St. Bernardino of Siena (1380-1444): A preacher born in Massa Marittima, he had the name of Jesus (or the abbreviation IHS) painted or carved wherever he went. He founded and lived in the Basilica dell'Osservanza in Siena, was beatified by Nicholas V in 1450 and proclaimed the patron saint of advertising in 1959 by Pope John XXIII.

St. Catherine of Siena (1347-80): Catherine Benincasa, an eloquent mystic, was responsible for bringing Pope Gregory XI back to Rome in 1377, thus breaking up the 'captivity' of the papacy in Avignon. She was canonized in 1461 and proclaimed patron saint of Italy by Pope Pius XII in 1939. See the Santuario e Casa di Santa Caterina (see SIENA-PALAZZI), incorporating her house and garden, and her father's dye-works.

San Gimignano: 38 km northwest of Siena. Pop: 7500. Tourist information: Palazzo del Popolo, Piazza della Cisterna. The best-preserved medieval hill town in Tuscany, surrounded by 13thC town walls. The main street, Via San Giovanni, leads to the two main *piazze*,

del Cisterna and del Duomo. The former contains the 13thC Palazzo del Popolo and Torre del Podestà. In the latter, triangular square are Palazzo Vecchio, Hotel Leon Bianco and a 13thC well. Round the corner is the Duomo or Collegiata di Santa Maria Assunta, built in 1148, but now much restored. Other sights include the 13thC Chiesa di Sant'Agostino and 14thC Rocca di Montestaffioli.
A combined L.6000 ticket entitles you to visit the Museo Civico (works by Lippi – see **A-Z** – and Gozzoli), Museo Etrusco (urns, oil and wine amphorae, coins and bronze mirrors), Museo di Arte Sacra (13th-14thC sculpture, and choral and sacred vestments) and the new Museo di Ornotologico, and climb the Torre del Podestà. All are open 0930-1230, 1500-1800 Tue.-Sun.
A smart new restaurant, La Mandragola, with a L.30,000 tourist menu, can be found in the ramparts at Via di Berignano 30-32. See **SAN GIMIGNANO-ATTRACTIONS**, **SIENA-EXCURSION**.

Sansepolcro: 39 km northeast of Arezzo. Pop: 16,000. Piero della Francesca's (see **A-Z**) home town. His famous *Resurrection* and *Madonna della Misericordia* are in the Museo Civico (0930-1300, 1430-1800 Wed.-Mon.; L.4500) at Via Aggiunti 65. The Hotel-Restaurant Il Fiorentino, Via L. Pacioli 60 (closed Fri.) is recommended.

Savonarola, Girolamo (1452-98): This Dominican friar and evangelical reformer attacked the corruption of the papacy from 1494 onwards, and was burnt at the stake as a heretic in Piazza della Signoria (see **FLORENCE-PIAZZE**) on 2 May 1498.

Sesto Fiorentino: 9 km northwest of Florence. Pop: 45,000. The town was founded on the six (*sesto*)-mile point along the old road from Florence to Pistoia. In 1735 the Marquis Ginori founded a ceramics factory here, and Museo della Porcellana di Doccia (0930-1300, 1530-1830 Tue.-Sat.; L.4000) charts its history. The 15thC Palazzo Pretorio has many coats of arms on its façade, and Palazzo Comunale (town hall) is a fine example of medieval Florentine architecture. The 15thC Villa Guicciardini in Corso Salviati, with its gardens, lakes and statues, is most imposing (check with the tourist office for opening times).

Siena: 68 km south of Florence. Pop: 65,000. Tourist information: Via di Vitti 43 and Piazza del Campo 55. The best parking is in the large football stadium near Santa Caterina church. This beautiful red-brick, red-tiled Gothic town – 'The City of the Virgin' – stands on three hills and is a complete contrast to Florence. Its elegant cockleshell Campo – scene of the ferocious Palio delle Contrade (see **Events**) – tunnelled alleyways, tall towers and *palazzi*, hidden gardens, wells and little squares, the glorious Palazzo Pubblico and Capella di Piazza are outstanding, as are the controversial striped-marble 12thC Duomo and

Torre del Mangia

a dozen other churches. Siena is the birthplace of many renowned artists, including Jacopo della Quercia, Francesco di Giorgio, Duccio di Buoninsegna and Simone Martini, whose works can be seen in the Pinacoteca Nazionale, Museo dell'Opera della Metropolitana del Duomo and Museo Civico. A first-class *pensione* is the Palazzo Ravizza, Pian dei Mantellini 34, which occupies a 17thC villa, while Albergo Chiusarelli, Via Curtatone 9, has palm trees and an air of faded gentility. Surrounded by 7 km of walls and with eight of the original 38 gates surviving, Siena has more charm than any other Tuscan town and should be visited by everyone at least once. See **SIENA**.

Signorelli, Luca (c. 1441-1523): Born in Cortona, this Tuscan painter influenced Michelangelo (see **A-Z**) and his work can be seen in the Museo Diocesano in Cortona (see **A-Z**), the abbey of Mte Oliveto Maggiore (see **Abbeys**) and Orvieto cathedral.

Vasari, Giorgio (1511-74): A Renaissance painter, architect and writer born in Arezzo. His book *Lives of the Most Excellent Italian Architects, Painters and Sculptors* was published in 1550. He trained under Andrea del Sarto in Florence, moved to Rome, helped decorate the Vatican, and returned to Florence to build the Uffizi (see **FLORENCE-MUSEUMS 1**) for Duke Cosimo I. He painted the frescoes in the great Salone dei Cinquecento, the parliamentary chamber of the Palazzo Vecchio (see **FLORENCE-PALAZZI**), and the tower of San Stefano dei Cavalieri (1569) in Pisa (see **PISA-ATTRACTIONS**), as well as the unusual gallery from the Uffizi across the Ponte Vecchio to Palazzo Pitti (see **FLORENCE-PALAZZI**). See **AREZZO-ATTRACTIONS**, **Renaissance**.

Viareggio: 27 km west of Lucca. Pop: 60,000. Tourist information: Viale Carducci 10. One of the oldest resorts in Italy, with a picturesque but sleazy canal port. The town is best known for its Feb. carnival with masked balls and firework processions with decorated floats, and for the beach where in 1822 Percy Bysshe Shelley was found drowned.

Volterra: 57 km west of Siena. Pop: 15,000. Tourist information: Via G. Turazza 2. This austere medieval walled town perched on a hill is worth a visit to see the superb 13thC Piazza dei Priori surrounded by grim palaces, the grey and white striped 12thC Duomo and baptistry, the sinister 500-year-old Fortezza Medicea (a prison), and the Museo Etrusco Guarnacci (0900-1300, 1430-1730 Tue.-Sun.) at Via Don Minzoni 11. There's also the Pinacoteca-Museo Civico at Via dei Sarti 1 and the Roman theatre and baths (combined ticket L.8000). A pleasant 2 km walk north to the cliffs of the Balze should also be considered. Alabaster is a major industry and the Cooperativa Artieri Alabastro has an excellent range of alabaster objects for sale. The hotels Nazionale and San Lino, and the restaurants Da Beppino and Il Porcellino are all good value.

Wine: Tuscan chianti has for decades been a cheap and cheerful red wine, and a favourite in Britain and many other countries. One hundred thousand Tuscans are employed in producing 850,000 hectolitres of chianti each year, 2.5% of which is chianti classico. The large Italian wine market is chaotic but is slowly being organized into more reliable and reputable quality designations. Of Italy's six DOCGs – the top-ranking Denominazione di Origine Controllata e Garantita – three come from Tuscany: Brunello di Montalcino, chianti classico (with a black cockerel logo) and Vino Nobile di Montepulciano. There are 250 DOGs in Italy, and notable Tuscan wines in this second category are Carmignano (from Montalbino), Pomino (from Rufina), Vernaccio di San Gimignano, Rosso di Montalcino and Rosso di Montepulciano. However, some of the lowest category – Vini da Tavola – such as Sassicaia, Solaia and Tavernelle, are now being strictly quality controlled. Decent white Tuscan wines are Vernaccia di San Gimignano and Montecarlo. Also look out for a good shipper's wine such as Antinori, Altesino, Avignonesi or Il Poggione. Recent good vintage years were 1978, 1982, 1983, 1985 and 1988 (but if the original wine was of poor quality a good vintage helps only marginally). You can arrange your own wine tour after discussing estate visits with the Chianti Classico Consorzio at Lungarno Corsini 4, Florence. In any case, try to visit the wine villages of Radda in Chianti, Greve in Chianti and Castellina in Chianti. See **FLORENCE-EXCURSION**, **Drinks**, **Wine Fairs**, **Wine Museums**.

tepulciano

Ponte Vecchio, Florence

Accidents & Breakdowns: In the event of an accident follow the usual procedure of exchanging names, addresses and insurance details. If someone is injured and you are held responsible, insist on contacting your embassy or consulate (see **A-Z**) as soon as possible.
In case of breakdowns, you should carry a red warning triangle (which can be hired from ACI (Automobile Club Italiano) offices – see **Driving**) with you at all times. This should be placed 50 m behind your vehicle before seeking help. Emergency telephones line motorways at 1 km intervals. Press the red button for medical assistance and the green button for breakdown assistance. Service and spare parts for Italian makes of car are easily obtainable; for other makes contact the relevant dealer in Florence. See **Emergency Numbers**.

Accommodation: The two main types of accommodation available in Tuscany are *pensioni* and hotels. *Pensioni* are generally cheaper, more informal and have fewer facilities than hotels in the same category but the service is usually of an equally high standard. More basic types of inn are known as *locande.*
The following figures indicate the price of a double room with bath in various categories of hotel (prices outside Florence tend to be lower): 5 star – L.250,000-500,000; 3 star – L.60,000-100,000; 1 star – L.35,000-50,000. Prices displayed in rooms (by law) are usually exclusive of breakfast but should include a service charge and taxes; check at the reception so you know exactly what you are paying for and report any discrepancies in your final bill to the tourist office.
It is necessary to book accommodation well in advance during the high season or major events (see **A-Z**). There is a day hotel (*albergo diurno*) at Florence station which rents rooms by the hour, where you can use the shower or Launderette facilities at a reasonable cost (0600-2000). See **Camping & Caravanning**, **Tourist Information**, **Villas**, **Youth Hostels**.

Airports: Galileo Galilei airport near Pisa (83 km west of Florence) is the region's international airport. Airport facilities include a restaurant, bar, information desk, duty-free shop and car-hire representatives. There is a rail-link (1 hr) to Florence's Santa Maria Novella station, also

known as Stazione Centrale; for details, tel: 216073. Most of the main airline companies operating from here have offices in Florence: British Airways, Via Vigno Nuovo 36r, tel: 218655; Alitalia, Lungarno Acciaivoli 10-12, tel: 27889. Tel: 050-28088 for flight information. Peretola civic airport at Val del Termine (5 km northwest of Florence) handles internal Alitalia flights as well as services to Nice, Brussels, Munich and Paris. Air UK, tel: 0345-666777, operates from Stansted and the Alisarda/Meridiana group, tel: 071-8392222, from Gatwick to Peretola. The airport runs an Alitalia bus-link to Santa Maria Novella station. Tel: 317123 for flight information.
There are small airports at Lucca, Siena and Grosseto.

Baby-sitters: Enquire at the hotel reception or ask your chambermaid. The tourist office may also be able to help. Expect to pay about L.10,000-15,000 per hr plus transport home. See **Children**.

Banks: See **Currency**, **Money**, **Opening Times**.

Best Buys: *Haute couture* in Florence is usually of a high quality but expensive. Hand-embroidered tablecloths and napkins make good presents, as do reproductions of famous statues or paintings. Via Tornabuoni is the elegant street where Gucci, Valentino and Ferragamo are to be found. Leathergoods are available in Via Calzaiuoli and Via Roma. Gold- and silversmiths are on the Ponte Vecchio. In Siena look out for wrought-iron objects, ceramics, and yellow and blue porcelain. Carrara has marble *objets d'art,* Volterra alabaster artefacts, Arezzo gold-plated work, linen and woollen sweaters, Pienza leatherware and ceramics, and in Pistoia – where you could once have purchased daggers and pistols – embroidery and lace. See **FLORENCE-SHOPPING**, **Markets**, **Shopping**.

Bicycle & Motorcycle Hire: As an alternative to driving a car, with all the interminable traffic jams and parking problems, hiring a bicycle makes sense. Details are available from Federazione Ciclistica Italiana, Piazza Stazione 2, Firenze (Florence), tel: 055-283926.
If you park your car for more than 2 hr in the car parks at Porta Romana, Piazza Vittorio Veneto, Piazza della Libertà, Piazza Cavalleggeri, Viale Mazzini or Piazza della Stazione, you will be entitled to the use of two free bicycles. For details contact Ciao & Basta

at Costa dei Magnoli 24, tel: 2342726, or the station, tel: 213307. Expect to pay about L.10,000 per day or L.40,000 per week for a bicycle. A deposit will be required. To use a scooter, you must be over 18 and hold a valid licence.
Other bicycle hire outlets:
Lucca: Cicli Rugeri, Piazza Santa Maria 32; Portoferraio, Elba: Alle Ghiaie, Via Cairoli 25-27; Siena: Autonoleggi Sartini, Via Pantaneto 27 (scooters).

Budget: 1992 prices.

Hotel breakfast	L.8000-12,000
Tourist menu (3 courses)	L.20,000-30,000
Dish of the day	L.8000-12,000
Wine	from L.4000 per bottle
Brandy	from L.4000 per glass
Coffee	L.1500-5000
Museum ticket	L.4000-12,000
Ice cream	L.1000-10,000

Buses: The ATAF bus company operates within Florence. Information, tickets and a free map can be obtained from its office at Piazza del Duomo 57r, tel: 212301. Tickets are also sold in bars (displaying ATAF stickers in the window) and tobacconists, and there are automatic ticket machines at some of the main stops in the centre. They cost L.800 for a single trip and L.1000 for journeys of up to 70 min. Books of eight tickets and passes are also available. Enter buses at the rear and validate your ticket in the machine by the door.
Several companies operate reasonably-priced services from Florence to the rest of Tuscany. There are frequent services by SITA, Via Santa Caterina da Siena 15r, tel: 211487, to Siena, Volterra and Arezzo, and LAZZI, Via della Stazione 1-6r, tel: 215154, to Lucca, Pisa, Prato and Pistoia. Contact the tourist office for details (see **Tourist Information**).
Main bus stations:
Arezzo: Viale Piero della Francesca; Lucca: Piazza Verdi; Pisa: Piazza Vittorio Emanuele II and Piazza Sant'Antonio; Prato: Piazza del Duomo; Siena: Piazza San Domenico.

Cameras & Photography: Film and other photographic equipment is available in Tuscany towns but does tend to be expensive. There are no restrictions on photography in the national museums but it is prohibited in municipal museums without prior authorization.

Camping & Caravanning: Details of all Tuscan camp sites can be obtained from Federazione Italiana del Campeggio, Casella Postale 649, 50100 Firenze (Florence). Information on camp sites on Elba is available from AAT, Calata Italia 26, Portoferraio.

Car Hire: Although driving in Florence is a penance, you may wish to rent a car for excursions. There are 10 companies, including Hertz, Avis and Inter-Rent, in the Borgo Ognissanti area. Hertz, Sartini, Avis and Autonoleggio all have offices in Siena, and Galileo Galilei airport at Pisa also has several car-rental desks. Ask for a discount when booking in advance. You will be asked to pay a deposit unless paying by credit card. You must be over 21 years of age and have held a licence for at least one year. Check the rates include unlimited mileage, breakdown service, maintenance and insurance but not petrol.

Chemists: Most chemists (*farmacia*) are open 0830/0900-1200/1300 and 1530/1600-1900/1930. A rota system ensures that at least one shop is open outside normal hours. See the *ore di turno* list in each chemist window or tel: 192 for details. See **Health**.

Children: See **Baby-sitters**, **Nature Reserves**.

Climate: The most pleasant times of the year to visit Tuscany are early summer and autumn. The weather in spring can be very changeable, while it can get quite cold in winter and oppressively hot and sticky at the height of summer. Rain is most frequent during the months of Nov., Jan. and April. Note that mosquitoes will be encountered on the coast.

Complaints: If you have been overcharged, ask to see the owner or manager of the premises. If you are still not satisfied, then you can report the establishment to the tourist office or the police (see **A-Z**).

Consulates:
UK – Lungarno Corsini 2, Firenze (Florence), tel: 284133.
USA – Lungarno Amerigo Vespucci 38, Firenze (Florence), tel: 298276.

Conversion Chart:

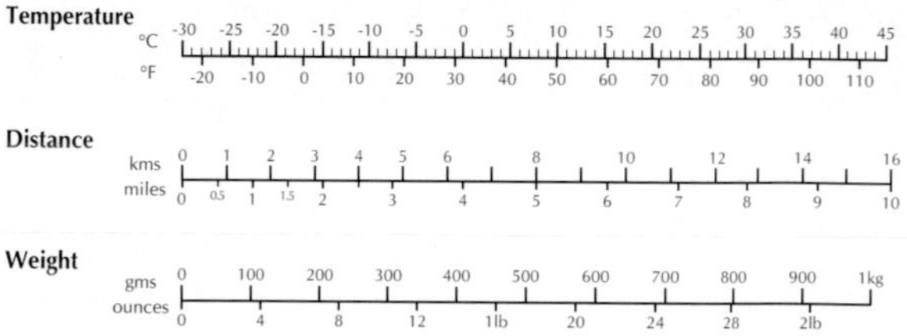

Temperature
°C -30 -25 -20 -15 -10 -5 0 5 10 15 20 25 30 35 40 45
°F -20 -10 0 10 20 30 40 50 60 70 80 90 100 110

Distance
kms 0 1 2 3 4 5 6 8 10 12 14 16
miles 0 0.5 1 1.5 2 3 4 5 6 7 8 9 10

Weight
gms 0 100 200 300 400 500 600 700 800 900 1kg
ounces 0 4 8 12 1lb 20 24 28 2lb

Crime & Theft: Keep all valuables and large amounts of cash in the hotel safe. Carry your wallet in a secure pocket and keep handbags under the arm as opposed to over the shoulder. In main towns consider wearing a money belt.
Never leave baggage unattended or visible in a locked car. Keep the serial numbers of your traveller's cheques separately (away from your cheque card) and make a note of your passport number.
If traveller's cheques are lost or stolen notify the originating office immediately. If you lose your passport notify the police and your consulate (see **A-Z**).
Carry car documents with you to prove ownership in case of theft. Keep a copy of police reports for insurance claims. See **Emergency Numbers**, **Insurance**, **Police**.

Currency: The lira is the Italian monetary unit (abbreviated as L., plural lire).
Coins – 10, 20, 50, 100, 200, 500 lire.
Notes – 1000, 2000, 5000, 10,000, 20,000, 50,000, 100,000 lire.
See **Money**.

Customs Allowances:

UK/EC	Cigarettes	Cigarillos	Cigars	Tobacco	Still Table Wine	Spirits/Liqueurs	Fortified Wine	Additional Still Table Wine	Perfume	Toilet Water	Gifts & Souvenirs
		or	or	or			or	or			
Duty Free	200	100	50	250 g	2 *l*	1 *l*	2 *l*	2 *l*	60 cc/ml	250 cc/ml	£32
Duty Paid	800	400	200	1 kg	90 *l**	10 *l*	20 *l*				

* Of which no more than 60 l should be sparkling wine.

Since 1 Jan. 1993 restrictions on allowances for duty-paid goods brought into the UK from any EC country have been abolished. Travellers are now able to buy goods, including alcoholic drinks and tobacco, paying duty and VAT in the EC country where the goods are purchased. However, duty-paid goods should be for the traveller's own use and carried by him personally. Whereas previously there were either-or options, travellers can now bring back the sum of the goods in the duty-paid column.

Disabled People: Tuscan towns are not easy to negotiate if you are wheelchair-bound. Most of the buildings are old and ill-equipped for the disabled, though a few have lifts. Contact the tourist office for a list of places catering for particular disabilities. See **Health**.

Drinks: Chianti wine is on sale in every restaurant. *Vino della casa* will be the cheaper house wine, while chianti classico, with the black cockerel symbol, is a reliable choice. Other alcoholic drinks include *vinsanto* (a fortified dessert wine), grappa (coarse colourless spirit) and *birra* (lager beer). The usual range of soft drinks is available. Most Tuscans prefer mineral water to the safe but chlorine-tasting tap water.

PASTICCERIA

Coffee is available in various forms: espresso is small and black, and cappuccino has frothy milk added in a larger cup. Italians rarely drink tea but it is usually available on request. See **Wine**.

Driving: Third-party insurance is obligatory when driving in Italy. Make sure you have your driving licence and car registration papers and that you are displaying a national identity sticker. You must also carry a red warning triangle in case of breakdowns (see **Accidents & Breakdowns**). The wearing of seat belts is compulsory.
Motorway (autostrada) tolls are quite expensive and vary by size of vehicle. Allow about L.40,000 from the French frontier at Ventimiglia to Florence for a Class 1 (small) car. Petrol coupons giving discounts on petrol, and motorway vouchers for use at motorway tolls, are available for foreign motorists bringing their cars into the country (but not if you hire a car in Italy).The ACI (Automobile Club Italiano) offers reciprocal membership to members of affiliated foreign automobile associations and will come to your aid if you have a breakdown. See **Car Hire**, **Parking**, **Petrol**.

Drugs: All drugs are illegal and there are severe penalties for offenders. Contact your embassy or consulate (see **A-Z**) if you are arrested for a drugs-related offence.

Eating Out: Tuscany has many restaurants (*ristoranti*), as well as *osterie, alberghi, trattorie* and *taverne*, offering food. Look for the *menu turistico*, a set-price three-course meal including a quarter of a bottle of wine and half a bottle of mineral water from prices as low as L.20,000, and even less in Arezzo and Prato. Self-service meals are available in the cities, and a *tavola calda* offers hot meals from a counter. Restaurant meals are divided into *primo* (antipasto, soup or pasta), *secondo* (main meat or fish dish) and *contorno* (vegetables). Lunch and dinner are identical in style and quantity. IVA (VAT) and *pane e coperto* (bread and cover charge) should be included in the price but service of 10% is usually extra. On the RESTAURANTS topic pages of this guidebook, Inexpensive meals are under L.25,000, Moderate under L.50,000 and Expensive over L.50,000. See RESTAURANTS by town, **Food**.

Electricity: 220 V. Small two-pin plugs are used; adaptors are available in Italy and the UK.

Emergency Numbers:

Carabinieri	112
Police	113
Fire	113/115 (Florence 222222)
Ambulance	113 (Florence 212222)
ACI breakdown service	116
Traffic police (Florence)	352141
Stolen cars service (Florence)	49771

Events: The main traditional festivals in Tuscany are:
February or March: Viareggio, Carnevale with processions, floats, masked balls, fireworks and a football tournament, until Shrove Tue.; Florence, Carnevale as above.
Easter Day: Florence, Lo Scoppio del Carro, burning of a cart laden with flowers and fireworks in Piazza del Duomo.
May: Massa Marittima, Balestro del Girifalco, joust of the falcon with crossbow shooting at a mechanical falcon in Piazza del Duomo and everyone in 15thC costume. Repeated 2nd Sun. in Aug.
June: Pisa, Regata di San Ranieri, boat races on the floodlit river Arno.
24 and 28: Florence, Gioco del Calcio Storico, traditional rough soccer game held in Piazza della Signoria, with all players in 16thC costume.
28: Pisa, Gioco del Ponte, a mock 16thC battle.
2 July: Siena, Palio delle Contrade, bareback horse race around Piazza del Campo dating from the 13thC, with costumed riders from Siena's 17 districts (*contrade*) competing for the *palio*, a banner showing the Madonna. Repeated 14 Aug. *25:* Pistoia, Giostra dell'Orso, 14thC joust of the bear in Piazza del Duomo.
July or August: Volterra, crossbow tournament in Piazza dei Priori.
15 August: Florence, Festa del Grillo, caged crickets are sold in Cascine park; Cortona, Sagra della Bistecca. *15-16:* Montepulciano, Il Bruscello, folklore and song festival.
1st Sun. in September: Arezzo, Giostra del Saracino, 13thC costumed jousting with eight armoured knights and much pageantry in Piazza

Grande. *7-8:* Florence, Festa della Rificolona, children's parades and races with lanterns from the Duomo to Santissima Annunziata. *14:* Lucca, Luminaria di Santa Croce, religious processions amid medieval buildings illuminated with torches.
See **Music**, **What's On**.

Gioco del Calcio Storico, Florence

Food: Tuscan cooking is as good as any in Italy. Each region has its specialities, and Florence is no exception, with *bistecca alla fiorentina* (grilled T-bone steak sprinkled with black pepper and olive oil), which is charged by weight in restaurants, *minestrone alla fiorentina* and *zuppa di fagioli alla fiorentina* (vegetable and bean soup, flavoured with rosemary, garlic, olive oil, onions and tomatoes). *Schiacciata alla fiorentina* is a vanilla sponge cake with many ingredients including olive oil (see **A-Z**). Siena, on the other hand, has a reputation for delicatessen dishes: *soppressate* (pork slices heavily spiced), *finocchiona* (minced pork with fennel), *capocolli* (pig's loin with spices) and *cinghiale* (wild boar with ginger or pepper). *La ribollita* is a stew of beans, bread and herbs. *Migliaccio senese* is a local black pudding. Pisa produces *cee*, a dish of young eels with garlic, sage and olive oil, and Pistoia *biroldo, roventini, rigaglia* and *cioncia* (pork delicacies). *Castagnaccio* is a cake made from Pistoian chestnuts, pine nuts and sultanas. In Livorno you will find *baccalà alla livornese* (salted cod with black olives, pepper and tomatoes) and *cacciucco alla livornese* (a fish stew with hot sauce). You will find tripe dishes available in every town; *il lampredotto* is tripe boiled with a green sauce and eaten as a sandwich, while plain *trippa* is cooked in onions and tomatoes. *Coniglio* (rabbit) is another popular dish. Tuscany also produces several cheeses, including *pecorino* (sheep cheese) and ricotta (buttermilk curd). See RESTAURANTS by town, **Eating Out**.

Guides: The official guide agency to Florence is Guide Turistiche at Viale Gramsci 9a, tel: 2478188. Agriturist, Piazza San Firenze 3, tel: 287838, organizes tours of Florence and the surrounding countryside.

Health: Before leaving the UK, you should obtain form E111 from the DSS, which entitles you to free medical treatment in Italy. Present it to any State doctor you consult, who will arrange for you to be exempted from payment. You should also take out a private health insurance policy to cover the cost of repatriation in case of serious illness. The tourist medical service in Florence operates 24 hr, manned by English- and French-speaking doctors at Via L. Il Magnifico, tel: 475411. There is a children's hospital, the Anna Meyer hospital, at Via L. Giordano 13, tel: 43991. See **Emergency Numbers**, **Insurance**.

Insurance: You should take out travel insurance covering you against theft, loss of property and money, as well as medical expenses, for the duration of your stay. Your travel agent should be able to recommend a suitable policy. See **Crime & Theft**, **Health**.

Laundries: Ask at your hotel for the nearest Launderette or use that at the day hotel at the station in Florence (see **Accommodation**). Prices are the same whether you have a service wash or do it yourself.

Lost Property: In Florence this can be claimed at Oggetti Ritrovati, Via Circondaria 19, tel: 367943 (0900-1200 Mon.-Sat.). Report any loss to the police immediately and get a copy of their report for insurance claims. Contact your consulate (see **A-Z**) if papers or documents are lost. Anything lost on trains can be retrieved in Florence from the lost property office in Santa Maria Novella station. If you lose your traveller's cheques, notify the issuing office immediately. See **Insurance**.

Maps: The best maps of Tuscany are the Touring Club Italiano *Toscana grande carta stradale d'Italia* at 1:200,000 or the Michelin map of northern Italy (No. 988). See **Orientation**.

Markets: Most towns have early-morning fruit, vegetable and flower markets, and on the coast, fish markets. Florence also has a straw goods market (Mercato del Porcellino) and a household goods market (Mercato di San Lorenzo). Flea markets are held in Piazza dei Ciompi, where coins, prints, stamps, postcards and bric-a-brac may be found. See **Best Buys**, **Shopping**.

lorence

Money: Foreign currency and traveller's cheques can be changed in banks and bureaux de change on the production of a passport. Major credit cards are widely accepted and many shops and hotels also accept payment by traveller's cheques or in foreign currency but often charge a high commission; check the rate they offer first. See **Crime & Theft, Currency.**

Music: Many Tuscan towns have notable music programmes. In Florence the Maggio Musicale festival is held mid May-June and features concerts, ballet and opera throughout the city. Tickets are available from the Teatro Comunale, Corso Italia 16. During the summer, concerts are held in the Boboli gardens, piazzas and cloisters. The opera season starts on 1 Oct. and continues through the winter. Other towns with significant musical programmes are: Fiesole, summer festival; Pisa, May and June; Siena, music week in Aug.; Pistoia, opera, ballet and concerts during July; and Lucca, Estate Musicale Lucchese, July-Sep., with Puccini operas performed in the Teatro del Giglio, as well as classical music concerts and jazz. See **Events**, **What's On**.

Nature Reserves:
The lake of Burano (1000-1500 Mon.-Wed. & Fri., Sep.-April) at Ansedonia, 45 km south of Grosseto, is the site of a bird sanctuary called Capalbio Scalo, sponsored by the Worldwide Fund for Nature.
Parco Naturale della Maremma (dawn-dusk Wed., Sat. & Sun.) at Alberese, 17 km south of Grosseto, can only be visited on foot to see the magnificent flora and fauna.
Oasi di Orbetello, 43 km south of Grosseto, tel: 0564-860239, is a sanctuary for birds migrating from the Adriatic to North Africa.
Isola di Montecristo is a nature reserve and can be reached from Portoferraio on Elba (see **A-Z**) during the summer.
Massaciuccoli nature park and reserve extends for 21,000 hectares along the coast between Livorno and Viareggio, west of Pisa.

Newspapers: Foreign newspapers and magazines are widely available in Tuscan towns at kiosks and newsagents. *La Nazione* is the daily Florence newspaper. *Firenze Oggi/Florence Today* (free) is bilingual and contains much useful information. See **What's On**.

Nightlife: Tuscan towns have a variety of bars, nightclubs, discos, theatres and music venues to suit all tastes. Teatro Comunale, Corso Italia 16, in Florence, presents productions of, among others, Pirandello, Puccini, Goldoni and Filippo. For movie-goers, there are cinemas in every town but these rarely show English-language films, except in Florence at the Astro cinema, Piazza San Simone. See FLORENCE-NIGHTLIFE, **Music**.

Opening Times: In general:
Banks – 0830-1330 Mon.-Fri. and sometimes 1445-1545. Some bureaux de change are open Sat. am and at Florence station 0830-1900.
Churches – 0730/0800-1200/1300, 1500/1530-1900.
Museums (State) – 0900-1400 (1300 Sun. & hols) Tue.-Sun. Private museums also open in the afternoons, including Mon. Note that last tickets are sold 30 min-1 hr before closing time.
Post offices – 0815-1330 Mon.-Fri., 0815-1200 Sat.
Shops – 0830/0900-1200/1300, 1530/1600-1900/1930 (food shops 1700-2000); closed Sun. and Sat. pm (summer), Mon. am (winter). Food shops close Wed. pm.

Orientation: Tourist offices will supply you with a free basic street map; all Tuscan towns are best explored on foot. See **Maps**.

Massa Marittima

Parking: Finding a space to park a car in most Tuscan towns is difficult. Use official car parks for reasons of security and convenience. Alternatively, park on the outskirts of town and walk, or take a bus or taxi to the centre. Illegally parked cars will be towed away. If this happens in Florence, go to the car pound at Via Circondaria 19, tel: 351562. See **Driving**.

Passports & Customs: A valid passport (or identity card for some EC visitors) is necessary but no visa is required for stays of less than three months. There is no limit on the amount of money you can take in or bring out of the country but amounts over one million lire must be declared on the V2 form you fill out on entry. Any valuable antiques or *objets d'art* must be accompanied by an authorization of purchase from the Fine Arts Department (arranged by the shop where you bought them). See **Customs Allowances**.

Petrol: Petrol stations are situated at frequent intervals along autostrade and at all town entrances/exits. Prices are clearly marked for *senza piombo* (lead-free) or *piombo,* and *super* or *normale*. Many pumps are attended, and for cleaning your windscreen, oil-testing or tyre-checking, a modest tip is appropriate. Some self-service pumps have a machine that accepts L.10,000 notes. See **Driving**.

Police: The *carabinieri* deal with serious crimes, the *polizia* are responsible for general crimes and crowd control, the *polizia stradale* are the road and traffic police and the *vigili urbani* deal with town traffic and administration.
Main police stations (*questura*):
Arezzo: Via Fra' Guittone; Florence: Via Zara 2; Lucca: Viale Cavour 38; Pisa: Via M. Lalli; Prato: Via Valentini; Siena: Via del Castoro.
See **Crime & Theft**, **Emergency Numbers**.

Post Offices: Stamps are sold at tobacconists displaying a T sign and at hotels, as well as post offices. Postboxes are coloured red. The main Florence post office has a 24 hr telegram and international telephone service, and poste restante facilities (0815-1900 Mon.-Fri., 0815-1300 Sat.).
Main post offices:
Arezzo: Via Guido Monaco 34; Florence: Via Pellicceria, off Piazza della Repubblica, and Via Pietrapiana 53-55; Lucca: Via Vallisneri; Pisa: Piazza Vittorio Emanuele II 8; Prato: Via A. Martini; Siena: Piazza G. Matteotti 36.
See **Opening Times**.

Public Holidays: 1 Jan., 6 Jan. (Epiphany), Easter Mon., 25 April (Liberation Day), 1 May (Labour Day), 15 Aug. (Assumption), 1 Nov. (All Saints' Day), 8 Dec. (Immaculate Conception), 25 Dec., 26 Dec.

Rabies: Still exists in Tuscany as in other parts of the Continent. As a precaution have all animal bites seen to immediately by a doctor.

Railways: Santa Maria Novella station in Florence has direct links to all the main Italian cities, including Rome, Naples and Genova, as well as to Paris and Zurich. Services are reliable and reasonably priced but as there are five categories of train (*super rapido* down to *locale*), supplements are charged. In some cases seat reservation is obligatory. Various discounts are available: *biglietto turistico*; *libera circolazione* (travel-at-will for 8-30 days); *chilometrico* (valid for 3000 km); one-month return; three-day return; and day return tickets. There are also family cards for at least three people and *Carta d'Argento* for the over-60s. In Florence, tel: 212319 for the left-luggage office and tel: 212296 for the railway police.

Religious Services (Florence): Church of England – St. Mark's, Via Maggio 1, tel: 294764 (0900 & 1030 Sun., 1000 Wed. & 2000 Fri.). American Episcopal Church – St. James', Via B. Rucellai 9, tel: 294417 (0800 & 1100 Sun.). Roman Catholic Masses in English are held at the Duomo (1700 Sat.) and the church of St. John of God, Borgo Ognissanti 16-20 (1000 Sun.).

Resorts: The Tuscan coastline has a score of popular resorts, some with sandy beaches, relatively clean sea, fish restaurants and evening entertainment. The best (or most sophisticated) are, from north to south, Forte dei Marmi, Viareggio (see **A-Z**), Marina di Pisa, Punta Ala facing Elba, Castiglione della Pescaia, Porto Santo Stefano and Porto Ercole (see **A-Z**).

Shopping: High-quality shops offering leatherware, jewellery, antiques and clothes are to be found in the centre of all Tuscan cities. Bargaining is a possibility and most shops can arrange to post your purchases abroad. See FLORENCE-SHOPPING, **Best Buys**, **Markets**.

Ski Resorts: In the Apennines northwest of Florence are three resorts: Abetone, Cutigliano and San Marcello Pistoiese. There are tourist offices in each resort which will provide information on facilities. There are also winter sports activities at Consuma, Stia and Vallombrosa in the mountains 40 km due east of Florence. The resort of Abbadia San Salvatore on Mte Amiata, 75 km south of Siena, has some 20 km of piste. Information can be obtained from Federazione Italiana Sport Invernali, Viale Matteotti 15, 50121 Firenze (Florence), tel: 055-576987.

Smoking: Smoking is not permitted in churches, museums, art galleries and theatres, and is discouraged in restaurants. Trains have separate non-smoking compartments.

Spas: For centuries health spas (*terme*) have been part of the Tuscan scene, often attended by Europeans seeking a cure. The most important spas are Montecatini Terme (see **A-Z**), Monsummano (near Montecatini), Saturnia and Chianciano Terme (see **AREZZO-EXCURSION**). Other spas include Bagni di Lucca (see **A-Z**), Casciana Terme, Equi Terme, Montioni and San Giuliano.

Sports: Spectator sports:
Horse racing and trotting races: Ippodromo Le Mulina, Viale di Pegaso, Cascine, tel: 411130, and Ippodromo Visaro, Piazzale della Cascine, tel: 360056, Florence. Club Ippico Senese, Località Pian del Lago,

tel: 53277, Siena.
Football: Stadio Comunale, Via M. Fanti 4-6, Florence.
Participatory sports:
Swimming: Most Tuscan towns have municipal pools.
Tennis: Municipal courts and clubs are available in every Tuscan town.
Golf: Golf Poggio Ugolino, Imprenuta, Strada Chiantigiana 3, Florence, tel: 2301096 (18-hole course but membership is required).
Riding: For details write to Federazione Italiana Sport Equestri, Via Paoletti 54, 50134 Firenze (Florence), tel: 055-480039.
Fishing: An inexpensive licence is required to fish in most lakes and rivers. For details write to Federazione Italiana della Pesca Sportiva, Via de' Neri 6, 50122 Firenze (Florence), tel: 055-214073.
Sailing: There are marinas at Cala Galera, Castiglione della Pescaia, Elba (see **A-Z**), Giannutri, Giglio Porto, Porto Ercole (see **A-Z**), Punta Ala, Talamone and Viareggio (see **A-Z**).
Skiing: See **Ski Resorts**.
Mountaineering: For details write to Club Alpino Italiano, Via Proconsolo 10, 50123 Firenze (Florence), tel: 055-216580.

Taxis: There are ranks outside all Tuscan railway stations and in the main squares of towns, where cars are allowed, including Pisa, Siena and Arezzo. Theoretically you cannot hail one but it is worth a try! They are yellow or white in colour, metred and usually expensive. There is an extra charge at night and for each item of luggage. In Florence, tel: 4390 or 4798; in Siena, tel: 49222 or 289350; and in Pisa, tel: 541600 or 41252. See **Tipping**.

Telephones & Telegrams: You will find public telephones on many streets, at railway stations, in bars and at newsagents displaying the blue and yellow sign, at the Centro Telefonici Pubblico (SIP) and in main post offices (see **A-Z**). New coin-operated telephones take 100, 200 and 500 lire coins. Other telephones operate on phonecards worth 1000 and 5000 lire, which can be purchased at tobacconists. However, some of the older ones still only accept tokens (*gettoni*) which can be purchased in bars, hotels, newsagents, tobacconists and post offices for L.200. It is best to make international calls from main

post offices where you pay at the end for the number of units used. To direct-dial abroad, dial 00 followed by the code for the country (UK – 44, USA – 1), then omit the first 0 of the city code.
There is a 24 hr telegram service at the head post office in Florence, or you can send a telegram by telephone by dialling 186. A cheaper, more efficient alternative is a night letter/telegram which is guaranteed to arrive the following morning.

Television & Radio: There are many TV and radio stations covering Tuscany but no English-language broadcasts.

Time Difference: 1 hr ahead of Greenwich Mean Time.

Tipping: Restaurant, café and hotel bills usually include a service charge but it is also customary to leave a small tip. Taxi drivers, cinema and theatre ushers, hairdressers and toilet attendants also expect to be tipped. Porters should be given L.1000 per item of luggage.

Toilets: Public toilets are scarce in Tuscany, though most museums and all railway stations will have them, as well as restaurants and a few of the larger stores. Most out-of-town petrol stations and all autostrade 'comfort' stops have toilets. However, be warned – standards of hygiene are usually abysmally low. *Signore* = Women; *Signori* = Men.

Tourist Information: Hotel reservations can usually be made at Ente Provinciale Turismo (EPT) offices and often at railway stations (Santa Maria Novella, Florence; Piazza della Stazione, Pisa). See individual town gazetteer entries for tourist office addresses. See **Guides**, **What's On**.

Transport: Rail and road services are generally good, although on many winding hill roads north of Florence a bus is advisable. Inter-city transport by train is fast, reliable and inexpensive. In towns, walk or book a coach tour departing from main hotels. If money is no object, you could hire a taxi or horse-drawn carriage. See **Airports**, **Buses**, **Railways**, **Taxis**.

attistero, Florence

Villas: Renting a modernized villa in an old wine estate in the centre of Tuscany makes for an agreeable holiday. For details try Tuscany – From Cottages to Castles at Tuscany House, 351 Tonbridge Rd, Maidstone, Kent, ME16 8NH, tel: 0622-726883.

What's On: Most tourist offices publish a seasonal newsletter of current events. *Firenze Oggi* in Florence appears six times a year and Siena has an annual brochure with events listed in English. Ask for a *calendario delle manifestazioni.* See **Events**, **Music**, **Newspapers**.

Wine Fairs:
16-20 May: Pontassieve, Toscanello d'Oro.
27 May-3 June: Montespertoli, chianti fair.
9-17 June: Cerreto Guidi-Vinci, chianti putto fair.
September: Greve in Chianti, chianti classico fair. *27-30:* Rufina, Baco Artigiano fair.
See **Wine**, **Wine Museums**.

Wine Museums: Before driving off into the Chianti vineyards it is worth visiting an *enoteca* (wine library/exhibition), two of which are at Palazzo dei Vini, Piazzi Pitti, Florence, tel: 055-213333, and Fortezza Medicea, Siena (see SIENA-ATTRACTIONS). Florence also has two others: Enoteca Nazionale di Giorgio Pinchiorri, Via Ghibellina 87, tel: 055-242777, and Enoteca Internazionale di Rham, Piazza della Santissima Annunziata 4, tel: 055-298849. See **Wine**, **Wine Fairs**.

Youth Hostels: For details write to Federazione Italiana Alberghi per la Gioventù, Viale Augusto Righi 2, Firenze (Florence).

This book was produced using QuarkXPress™ and Adobe Illustrator 88™ on Apple Macintosh™ computers and output to separated film on a Linotronic™ 300 Imagesetter

Text: Patrick Delaforce
Photography: Philip Enticknap
Electronic Cartography: Bartholomews

First published 1993

Published by HarperCollins Publishers
Printed in Hong Kong
ISBN 0 00 435924-0

Guidebook information is subject to being outdated by changes to opening hours, prices, and by fluctuating restaurant standards. Every effort has been made to give you an up-to-date text but the publishers cannot accept any liability for errors, omissions or changes in detail or for any consequences arising from the use of information contained herein.
The publishers welcome corrections and suggestions from readers; write to: The Publishing Manager, Travel Guides, HarperCollins Publishers, PO Box, Glasgow G4 0NB.